Preferring Justice

Preferring Justice

Rationality, Self-Transformation, and the Sense of Justice

Eric M. Cave

WestviewPress

A Division of HarperCollins*Publishers*

Copyright © 1998 by Westview Press, A Division of HarperCollins Publishers, Inc.

Published in 1998 in the United States of America by Westview Press, 5500 Central Avenue, Boulder, Colorado 80301-2877, and in the United Kingdom by Westview Press, 12 Hid's Copse Road, Cumnor Hill, Oxford OX2 9JJ

A CIP catalog record for this book is available from the Library of Congress.
ISBN 0-8133-2808-X

The paper used in this publication meets the requirements of the American National Standard for Permanence of Paper for Printed Library Materials Z39.48-1984.

10   9   8   7   6   5   4   3   2   1

In memory of Gregory Stephen Kavka,
who taught me that some of the
finest people on this earth are Hobbesians

Contents

Tables and Figures

Tables

Figures

Preface and Acknowledgments

From the individual point of view, the sense of justice appears to do no more than to limit what individuals can do in pursuit of their ends and open them to exploitation. Realizing this, we might each wonder whether the sense of justice is anything more than an instrument of social control, something we would each be better off without. We can retire such doubts by showing that flawed agents of differing abilities choosing under partial information would advance maximally those of their ends having nothing to do with justice by maintaining such a disposition. And that is just what I propose to do here.

This manuscript began in 1994 as my dissertation in the Department of Philosophy at the University of California, Irvine. Its structure and arguments have changed dramatically in the several years I have spent on it since then, and I hope that it is the better for these changes.

I owe a tremendous debt of gratitude to Greg Kavka, who chaired my dissertation until his death in February, 1994. He was incredibly generous with his time and energy even when he had little to spare. Without his advice, criticism, and unflagging support, personal and professional, this manuscript would never have been. Indeed, I would not have been capable of writing it. I miss him keenly.

With respect to the final version of this manuscript, I owe almost as much to Duncan MacIntosh, who read an earlier incarnation of it for Westview Press. His thoughtful, detailed, and incisive evaluation of my project set new standards for supererogation in refereeing. And as if that were not enough, he reread several sections of it that I had revised in response to his criticisms and comments. I have indicated the most significant of these in the notes to the manuscript, but scarcely a page of it has not benefitted from his efforts.

I thank Alan Nelson and Gary Watson for reading early versions of this work in their entirety, and for valuable comments on them. Chris Morris read multiple drafts of several chapters and provided me with very useful feedback. He has also been a constant source of support and encouragement for me. For valuable comments on one or more chapters, I thank David Estlund, Ned McClennen, Gerry Santas,

Bruno Verbeek, and anonymous referees for the *Canadian Journal of Philosophy* and *Dialogue*.

I have benefitted from discussing some of the issues treated here with Chuck Carr, Ron Endicott, Bill Harms, Joe Sartorelli, David Schmidtz, David Shoemaker, and Peter Vanderschraaf. Thank you all.

Over the last several years, I have presented material from this manuscript at the University of California, Irvine, Union College, the University of Waterloo, the meetings of the American Philosophical Association, Pacific Division, and the Mid-South Philosophy Conference. Thanks to those who listened for their questions, comments, and suggestions.

Arkansas State University supported part of my research on the sense of justice with a Faculty Research Grant during summer, 1996. Part of this grant, along with a grant from the Nathan Deutsche Foundation, helped to cover some of the expenses involved with typesetting this manuscript. Richard McGhee, Dean of Arts and Sciences at Arkansas State University, came through for me not once but twice when I was desperately short of the funds required to bring it to press. And during my last year of work on *Preferring Justice*, Chuck Carr, in his capacity as my department chair, provided me with a much-needed course release and kept departmental demands on my time to a minimum. For all of this support from my home institution, I am deeply grateful.

A forerunner of Chapter 7 appeared as "The Individual Rationality of Maintaining a Sense of Justice" in *Theory and Decision* 41 (1996): 229–56. I draw upon this article here with kind permission from Kluwer Academic Publishers. Sections of Chapter 9 appear as "Habituation and Rational Preference Revision" in *Dialogue* 37 (1998). I am grateful to *Dialogue* for the permission to use this material.

And finally, heartfelt thanks to Alyson Gill and Emily Bunting, each of whom in her own distinctive way has helped me to remember that some of the most valuable things in life have nothing to do with the writing of books. Without their love and support, I would have been very much the poorer during the years I spent working on this one.

1

Introduction:
A Reconciliation Project

At least since Plato's *Republic*, there has been a strand in ethics dedicated to reconciling moral requirements with the requirements of reason. Typically, such reconciliation projects have sought to show that particular sets of moral constraints are consistent with reason. I propose a twist on this project: let us try to show that reason requires individuals to maintain the sense of justice.

To do so is distinct from moving them to become just. Arguments, after all, can only show individuals that they ought to accept conclusions, and there may well be a gap between understanding and motivation. We seek to justify the sense of justice to individuals, although we shall do what we can to make this justification motivationally effective.

We cannot expect showing someone that there are reasons to maintain the sense of justice which she does not recognize as such to have any effect on her motivation. Thus, as our concern to develop a motivationally effective justification of the sense of justice requires, we shall provide individuals with reasons to maintain such a disposition which each recognizes as such from her own perspective.

Such justification is always directed to an audience. Narrowly speaking, we address philosophically-inclined inhabitants of the United States during the late twentieth century. As we shall see, however, it has implications for any community characterized by substantial agreement on rules of justice, but pluralism when it comes to conceptions of the good life.

A Minimal Conception of the Sense of Justice

Let individuals occupy the *circumstances of justice* if two conditions obtain. First, their conceptions of the good life must be partially competitive. Maximal satisfaction of the preferences of each must rule out maximal satisfaction of the preferences of at least some others.[1] And second, cooperation must pay. Each must expect to satisfy her own preferences more fully interacting with others than acting alone.

To the extent that each wants to see her preferences satisfied as fully as possible, her interests conflict with those of at least some of her fellows. And to the extent that each wants to interact with her fellows to enhance her own expectations, her interests cohere with those of her fellows. Thus, the circumstances of justice define a partial conflict of interests.[2] Let a *conception of justice* be any set of rules by means of which individuals occupying the circumstances of justice resolve this conflict.

Let the *sense of justice* be the disposition to comply with these rules rather than violating them just because one values doing so intrinsically. Then possession of the sense of justice involves two conditions. First, an individual must be disposed to choose just over unjust actions. Call this the *compliance condition.* Second, an individual must be disposed to choose just over unjust actions for the right reason, because she values doing so intrinsically. Call this the *motivation condition.*

If someone is not disposed to choose justice over injustice, she is amoral or unjust. And if someone chooses to act justly rather than unjustly for purely instrumental reasons, she is opportunistic, not just. Thus, taken together, the compliance and motivation conditions define a minimal conception of the sense of justice.

Sometimes, "sense of justice" is used more narrowly than this, to describe a disposition involving certain emotions as well as behavioral and motivational components.[3] But while not all conceptions of the sense of justice involve an emotive element, the compliance and motivation conditions are common to virtually all such conceptions. Further, possession of the minimal sense of justice grounds enough benefits that the question of whether maintaining one is rational should interest even those committed to an emotively thick sense of justice. Hence, we shall concern ourselves exclusively with the minimal sense of justice. And from this point on, we shall restrict the meaning of "sense of justice" accordingly.

Fundamental Justification of the Sense of Justice

A *fundamental* justification of a given domain is an evaluation of that domain in terms of standards entirely outside of that domain.[4] Any given evaluation is fundamental only relative to some set of standards, so that by appealing to different sets of standards, it may be possible to provide separate and compatible evaluations of the same domain.

To provide individuals with a fundamental justification of the sense of justice is to provide them with reasons for maintaining this disposition which do not derive from this disposition itself. A demonstration that instrumental rationality requires individuals to maintain the sense of justice, for example, would constitute a fundamental justification of this disposition. For contrast, consider Rawls' claim that possession of the sense of justice enables individuals to participate in a well-ordered society.[5] Since one of the defining features of a well-ordered society is the exercise of a common sense of justice, no justification of the sense of justice appealing to this claim would be fundamental.

We seek to provide members of our audience with a fundamental justification of the sense of justice. While we cannot realistically hope to provide all of them with such a justification, the closer we come to doing so, the more fully we succeed at our project.

Why a Fundamental Justification of the Sense of Justice Matters

Most of us exhibit the sense of justice. And most of us seek to reinforce this disposition in those for whom we care. If pressed, we typically defend these practices by linking possession of the sense of justice to individual good: crime does not pay, cheating Joes always show, time wounds all heels.[6]

But we are sometimes tempted by injustice, even those of us exhibiting the sense of justice. Other times, by acting justly, we enable others to exploit us for a loss. Reflecting on the sense of justice, an individual may realize that she need not exhibit the sense of justice herself to benefit from her fellows possessing such a disposition. And she may realize that having the sense of justice is costly to her, both in terms of missed opportunities and an increased risk of being exploited by others. Realizing these things, she may come to doubt that she has sufficient reason to maintain the sense of justice.

Plagued by such doubts, even a just individual must regard the sense of justice with suspicion, wondering whether she ought to retain it. Such alienation from the sense of justice may undermine its effectiveness in determining behavior, causing affected individuals to act justly less often, and unjustly more often, than they did previously. And this constitutes a threat to us all.

Suppose that, as a result of such doubts, some of the just members of our community were to become alienated from the sense of justice. These would violate rules of justice more often than they did before becoming alienated. The resulting increase in unjust behavior among us would inspire more doubts about the sense of justice, alienating more just individuals from it, and causing a further increase in unjust behavior. This increase would inspire even more doubts about the sense of justice, and so on, until every one of us exhibiting the sense of justice was alienated from it. In this way, unanswered doubts about the sense of justice could transform a community in which few were alienated from this disposition into one in which all were so alienated.

Such a transformation would worsen the expectations of every one of us relative to her expectations were few of us alienated from the sense of justice. For were all of us so alienated, just individuals would cooperate less frequently than were few of us so alienated. Cooperating less frequently, each would realize a diminished return on her cooperative efforts. And with less to gain from exploiting just individuals, unjust individuals would each realize a diminished return on her predatory efforts as well. Thus, everyone within our community, just and unjust, would do worse were all of us alienated from the sense of justice than were some of us so alienated.

A fundamental justification of the sense of justice can allay the doubts causing such alienation by revealing that each of us has sufficient reason to maintain such a disposition. And only such a justification can do so. For anything short of such a justification would reveal reasons for affirming the sense of justice which are no less suspect than this disposition itself.

The more doubts about the sense of justice we can answer, the less likely we all are to end up alienated from this disposition. Thus, to the extent that we succeed at our project, we decrease our odds of realizing an outcome on which each of us would be worse off than she presently is. And thus, our project should matter to members of our audience because the expectations of each are bound up, to some extent, with its success.

But perhaps we have already realized the outcome success at our project would help to forestall. Indeed, if the doomsayers among us are to be believed, we are all alienated from the sense of justice already. Perhaps most of us, as the result of such alienation, have already rid ourselves of it entirely. One might worry that it is just too late for our project to have any effect within our community.

But this worry is unfounded, even if we turn out to be at some advanced stage of alienation from the sense of justice already. For besides preventing such alienation, a fundamental justification of the sense of justice can disalienate individuals from this disposition, even inspire unjust individuals to become just.[7] By accomplishing either of these things, it would increase the frequency of cooperation within our community. Cooperating more frequently, just individuals would realize an increased return on their cooperative efforts. And with more to gain from exploiting just individuals, unjust individuals would realize increased returns on their predatory efforts as well. Thus, even were we already alienated from the sense of justice, the success of our project would benefit many of us.

Such success would not necessarily benefit all of us, however. For alienated and unjust individuals may profit by acting unjustly. Such individuals would benefit from our project only if they gained more from the increased cooperation generated by its success than they lost in acting justly instead of unjustly. Any who lost more than they gained from this would be harmed by our project, not benefitted by it. But our project should matter no less to those who might be harmed by it than to those who might be benefitted by it. Thus, that our project might harm some members of our audience does not reduce its significance for them.

Any who lost as much as they gained, and no more, in being restored or converted to justice would be neither benefitted nor harmed by our project. Its success would have no significance for those who could identify themselves positively as members of this class.

But the constitution of this class depends upon how much of a cooperative increase our project generates. And this, in turn, depends upon just how successful it is. Thus, before we have succeeded or failed at our project, individuals cannot determine positively whether or not they belong to the class of those who would be neither benefitted nor harmed by our project. And thus, even realizing that she may be a member of this class, each must regard our project as a potential source of benefit or harm to her, at least until we are done with it.

And once we are done with our project, the constant turnover within our community precludes even those whom it has not affected from regarding it with indifference. For in the course of such turnover, the class of individuals affected by our project may change. Thus, members of our community must always regard our project as a potential source of harm or benefit.

And so, in a community characterized by widespread alienation from the sense of justice, a fundamental justification of such a disposition may not benefit everyone. But even so, the expectations of all are still bound up, for better or for worse, with the success of our project. Thus, even were most or all of us alienated from the sense of justice, our project would retain its significance for us.

Communitarian Worries About Our Project

If we are distinct from our values ontologically, then we can imagine ourselves questioning these values. And for the reasons we have suggested, we should expect some of us, at least, to question the sense of justice. But on a communitarian understanding of ourselves, such questioning makes no sense.

Communitarians suggest that we are constituted by our values, and that these are given to us entirely by our various roles within our community.[8] Were this so, then the sense of justice would not be something we each possess, but a part of who we each are. But in this case, were I to become a person lacking the sense of justice, the person I would have become would no longer be me. For with the loss of my sense of justice, I would have ceased to exist. Talk of a case in which I lacked the sense of justice would commit us to the claim that I would exist in such a case and the claim that I would not exist in such a case, which is impossible. So understanding ourselves, those of us exhibiting the sense of justice could not conceive ourselves as lacking it, so alienation from this disposition would not be a problem for us. We would, thus, have no need of a fundamental justification of the sense of justice.

Were this reasoning correct, none of us would ever have become alienated from the sense of justice in the first place.[9] But we have explained how we might come to frame the doubts that cause such alienation. And alienation from the sense of justice is a problem within our community, although we disagree about its extent. Thus, our project cannot be dismissed as the solution to a problem generated entirely by mistaken assumptions about the self.

Perhaps, however, communitarians can admit our alienation from the sense of justice, and even propose a remedy for it, without acknowledging the significance of our project. Because we are under the sway of a false ideology of the self, namely atomism, we fail to see the contradiction involved in imagining ourselves without the sense of justice. By appealing to this false ideology, we frame skeptical doubts about this disposition, which alienate us from it. To dispel this alienation, communitarians might argue, we should not propagate atomism by justifying the sense of justice to individuals. Rather, we should do away with the false ideology causing alienation, showing individuals that they ought to exchange an atomistic conception of the self for the communitarian one.

To sustain this challenge to our project, communitarians must provide a justification of their conception of the self which is both effective at disalienating individuals from the sense of justice and distinct from our proposal for doing so. But no such justification can be constructed.

Communitarians might justify their conception of the self by appealing to the sense of justice itself. But in the face of such a justification, any doubts an alienated individual had about the sense of justice would translate directly into doubts about the communitarian conception of the self. And doubting the adequacy of this conception of the self, an individual would remain alienated from all of its elements, including the sense of justice.

Alternatively, communitarians might justify their conception of the self to individuals without appealing to the sense of justice. But since the sense of justice is an element of the communitarian conception of the self, to do so is just to offer them a fundamental justification of this disposition. But if this is so, then an appeal to communitarianism fails to establish that we can disalienate individuals from the sense of justice without providing them a fundamental justification of this disposition.

Although communitarians can diagnose alienation from the sense of justice by appealing to their conception of the self, they cannot provide us an effective means for dispelling it distinct from the one we propose to develop. And to the extent that they recognize such alienation as a problem for us, actual or potential, even communitarians must acknowledge our need to disalienate individuals from the sense of justice. Thus, appearances to the contrary, an appeal to communitarianism fails to undermine our project.

Internalist Worries About Our Project

Moral internalism asserts a conceptual connection between morality and either motivation or reasons for action.[10] Moral externalism is the denial of moral internalism. Were some form of externalism true, we would have to appeal to more than just the concept of morality to provide individuals with reasons to act justly. Thus, externalists who locate us within the circumstances of justice must recognize the significance of our reconciliation project. It is not so clear, however, that internalists must do so.

Formulated as a thesis about motivation, internalism asserts that by their very nature, moral considerations motivate agents to act morally. Different forms of internalism about motivation describe the connection between morality and motivation differently. But were moral obligation, or moral judgement, or the recognition of a moral obligation enough to motivate agents to act morally, we would not have to provide them a fundamental justification of the sense of justice to motivate them to act justly. They would do so because they were obligated to do so, or because they judged they were obligated to do so, or because they recognized they were obligated to do so.

But even were there a conceptual connection between morality and motivation, our project would still benefit us. For reflection might still generate skeptical doubts about the sense of justice. Such skeptical doubts might still alienate us all from the sense of justice, rendering each of us worse off than she would be in the absence of such alienation. And by reducing our odds of realizing this outcome, a fundamental justification of the sense of justice would yet benefit us. Thus, an appeal to internalism about motivation fails to undermine our project.

But where an appeal to internalism about motivation fails, an appeal to internalism about justification might succeed. Formulated as a thesis about justification, internalism asserts that by their very nature, moral considerations provide agents with reasons for action. If this were so, then moral considerations themselves would provide agents reasons for acting justly sufficient to answer any skeptical doubts about the sense of justice. And we would not require a fundamental justification of the sense of justice to disalienate individuals from this disposition. We shall consider separately the implications of the dominant variants of internalism about justification for our project.

According to *agent* internalism, moral obligations necessarily provide those whom they obligate with reason to do the right thing.[11] *Weak* agent internalism asserts that moral obligations necessarily provide agents with reasons for action, but not always overriding ones. Such internalism poses no threat to our project. For even were it true, disalienating individuals from the sense of justice would still require us to show that the balance of reasons supports maintaining this disposition. But an appeal to *strong* agent internalism, which asserts that moral obligations necessarily provide agents with overriding reasons for action, might undermine our project.[12]

Were strong agent internalism true, then by their very nature, rules of justice would provide those obligated by them with sufficient reason to act justly. Assuming that we are all obligated by rules of justice, none of us could sustain the doubts causing alienation from the sense of justice. And in the absence of such doubts, we would have no need of a fundamental justification of the sense of justice.

Were this reasoning correct, we would never have become alienated from the sense of justice in the first place. But evidently, some of us have. Thus, our project cannot be dismissed as the solution to a problem generated entirely by mistaken assumptions about the connection between moral obligation and reasons for action.

Perhaps the strong agent internalist can acknowledge our evident alienation from the sense of justice. If rules of justice did not obligate us all, then even given the truth of strong agent internalism, at least some of us could sustain the doubts causing alienation from the sense of justice. But once she admits the possibility of such alienation, the strong agent internalist can no longer dismiss our project as insignificant. For where such alienation exists or might come to exist, offering individuals a fundamental justification of the sense of justice affects their expectations in all of the ways we have indicated.

According to *appraiser* internalism, the judgement that she is morally obligated provides an agent with reason to do the right thing.[13] Weak appraiser internalism could be true, and we would still have to show individuals that the balance of reasons favors the sense of justice to disalienate them from it. But an appeal to strong appraiser internalism might undermine our project.

Were strong appraiser internalism true, only those who deny that rules of justice obligate them could become alienated from the sense of justice. And we could disalienate them from this disposition by bringing them to believe that these rules obligate them. For so believing, each would have sufficient reason to act justly rather than unjustly, so she could sustain no skeptical doubts about the sense of justice. And were we able to disalienate individuals from the sense of justice by correcting their beliefs, we would have no need for a fundamental justification of the sense of justice.

But a justification of the belief that rules of justice obligate alienated individuals must either appeal to the sense of justice or not. If the former, it could not disalienate such individuals from the sense of justice, for it could not retire their doubts about this disposition. And if the latter, then given the truth of strong appraiser internalism, such a justification would constitute a fundamental justification of the sense of justice. For by showing an individual that she has sufficient reasons to act justly rather than unjustly without appealing to the sense of justice, we would provide her sufficient reasons to maintain any disposition which would cause her to consistently choose just over unjust actions. And these reasons would not themselves derive from the sense of justice.

According to *hybrid* internalism, recognizing that she is morally obligated provides an agent with reason to do the right thing.[14] If an agent has an obligation to act justly, and she realizes she has such an obligation, then she has reason to do as rules of justice require. Weak hybrid internalism could be true, and we would still have to show individuals that the balance of reasons favors the sense of justice to disalienate them from it. But an appeal to strong hybrid internalism might undermine our project.

Were strong hybrid internalism true, we could disalienate individuals obligated by rules of justice from the sense of justice merely by bringing them to realize that they are so obligated. We would, thus, appear to have no need for a fundamental justification of the sense of justice.

But a justification of the claim that alienated individuals are obligated by rules of justice must either appeal to the sense of justice or not. If the former, it could not disalienate individuals from the sense of justice, for it could not retire their doubts about this disposition. And if the latter, then given the truth of strong hybrid internalism, such a justification would constitute a fundamental justification of the sense of justice, for the same reason that it would constitute such a justification were appraiser internalism true.

Thus, no version of internalism about justification can provide us an effective means for disalienating individuals from the sense of justice distinct from the one we propose to develop. And to the extent that proponents of such internalism recognize alienation as a problem for us, they must acknowledge our need to disalienate individuals from the sense of justice. Thus, an appeal to internalism about justification fails to undermine our project.

And thus, whichever of moral externalism and moral internalism is true, our reconciliation project matters. Since both are controversial theses, that our project presupposes the truth of neither advantages it. So as to retain this advantage, we shall remain agnostic about whether or not there is a necessary connection between moral considerations and either motivation or justification.

Preview of the Main Argument

In Chapter 2, I propose to justify the sense of justice to members of our audience by arguing that unjust contractors occupying an appropriate choice situation would choose to transform themselves into just ones. After discussing the conditions under which such an argument would constitute a fundamental justification of the sense of justice, I articulate and defend its major components.

The first of these is a set of contractors resembling us but for their lack of the sense of justice. The second is a two-stage choice situation in which these contractors must choose and execute a joint strategy for implementing some designated conception of justice, then choose individual strategies for satisfying their preferences within the context defined by their joint strategy choice. And the third is an instrumental conception of rationality.

The choice situation occupied by our contractors involves uncertainty, and there is some controversy about what instrumental rationality requires of agents under uncertainty. To resolve this controversy, I formulate a short list of decision rules for choice under uncertainty which includes the maximin principle, the disaster avoidance principle, and the expected utility principle. After defending the adequacy of this list, I employ a creation of Robert Nozick's, the decision value framework, to adjudicate between the demands of the rules comprising this list.[15]

In Chapter 3, I describe in detail my proposal that contractors transform themselves from unjust into just individuals. Understanding self-transformation in terms of the revision of intrinsic preferences, I identify possessing the sense of justice with exhibiting a certain preference ordering over outcomes, a set of principled preferences, and argue for the adequacy of this identification. To clarify this account of the sense of justice, I differentiate it from a number of recent proposals for understanding the relationship between rationality and morality.

Chapter 4 contains an argument for the collective rationality of self-transformation. To establish that each of our contractors would do better if all transformed themselves than if all did not, I narrow their available joint strategies for implementing rules of justice to two: the policer strategy and the transformer strategy. Policers implement rules of justice by setting up an enforcement mechanism to punish violations of these rules. Transformers implement rules of justice by agreeing to develop principled preferences, then empowering an enforcement mechanism to induce one another to comply with this agreement. By appealing to benefits peculiar to a community of individuals possessing principled preferences, I argue that each of our contractors would do better at satisfying her preferences among transformers than among policers. And by appealing to this conclusion, and the structure of our choice situation, I argue that our contractors would choose the transformer over the policer strategy, then execute it.

Having executed the transformer strategy, our contractors must select an individual strategy for pursuing their preferences within the context created by their so doing. I narrow the set of their available individual strategies to two: the true transformer strategy and the faker strategy. True transformers develop principled preferences, while fakers merely pretend to develop such a preference ordering. In Chapter 5, I apply the maximin principle to the choice between these two strategies. In Chapter 6, I analyze this choice in terms of the disaster avoidance principle. And in Chapter 7, I bring the expected utility principle to bear upon this choice.

Chapter 8 integrates the results of Chapters 5, 6, and 7. Here, I argue that to maximize decision value, most of our contractors must choose the true transformer over the faker strategy. On this basis, I conclude that instrumental rationality requires most of them to transform themselves. I close the chapter by considering some objections to this conclusion.

If our contractors could not alter their intrinsic preferences, the conclusion of Chapter 8 would be threatened. For given any two alternatives, the one required of an agent by instrumental rationality must be one which she is capable of choosing. In Chapter 9, I answer the objection that self-transformation is impossible for rational agents, and thus irrational for our contractors.

In the concluding chapter, I entertain several objections to the claim that our argument for the rationality of self-transformation constitutes a fundamental justification of the sense of justice. After answering these objections, I consider the most significant limitations of this justification, then close by considering the prospects for overcoming these.

Notes

1. I borrow this way of describing the objective component of the circumstances of justice from David Gauthier. See David Gauthier, "Value, Reasons, and

the Sense of Justice," in *Value, Welfare, and Morality*, ed. R. G. Frey and Christopher Morris (Cambridge: Cambridge University Press, 1993), 190–1.

2. Duncan MacIntosh argues that questions of justice also arise within (some) complete conflicts of interest. If this is so, then to fully reduce justice to rationality, one would have to show that rationality can resolve (some) complete conflicts of interest. But we are not engaged in such a reduction, so we can set this problem aside. See Duncan MacIntosh, "Categorically Rational Preferences and the Structure of Morality," in *Vancouver Studies in Cognitive Science*, vol. 7, ed. Peter Danielson (Vancouver: Oxford University Press, 1996), 281–301.

3. See, for instance, John Rawls, *A Theory of Justice* (Cambridge: Harvard University Press, 1971), 485–90. Or see David Gauthier, *Morals by Agreement* (New York: Oxford University Press, 1986), 326–9.

4. For discussions of fundamental justification, see Robert Nozick *Anarchy, State and Utopia* (New York: Basic Books, Inc., 1974), 6–9; Robert Nozick, *Philosophical Explanations* (Cambridge: Harvard University Press, 1981), 632–4; and Peter Danielson, *Artificial Morality* (London: Routledge, 1992), 19–38.

5. See Rawls, 525–7.

6. The first of these sayings is commonplace. The second I learned from my grandfather. And the third I learned from Greg Kavka, his gloss of Hobbes' reply to the Foole.

7. For the notion of disalienation, see Richard B. Brandt, *A Theory of the Good and the Right* (New York: Clarendon Press, 1979), 186–7.

8. See, for instance, Michael Sandel, *Liberalism and the Limits of Justice* (Cambridge: Cambridge University Press, 1982), 150. See also Alasdair MacIntyre, *After Virtue: A Study in Moral Theory* (London: Duckworth Press, 1981), 201–5. And see the discussion of communitarianism in Will Kymlicka, "Liberalism and Communitarianism," *Canadian Journal of Philosophy* 18 (1988): 181–204.

9. For a more general version of this argument, see Jan Narveson, "Reason in Ethics—or Reason versus Ethics?" in *Morality, Reason, and Truth: New Essays on the Foundations of Ethics*, ed. David Copp and David Zimmerman (Totowa: Rowman and Allanheld, 1985), 235.

10. In the following discussion, I employ the classification of moral internalism developed in David O. Brink, *Moral Realism and the Foundations of Ethics* (New York: Cambridge University Press, 1989), 37–43. A similar classification can be found in Stephen L. Darwall, "Internalism and Agency," *Philosophical Perspectives* 6 (1992): 155–74.

11. For a discussion of agent internalism, see Brink, 40. See also the discussion of constitutive existence internalism in Darwall, 157–8.

12. For more on the distinction between weak and strong internalism, see Brink, 41–2.

13. For a discussion of appraiser internalism, see Brink, 40. See also the discussion of judgement internalism in Darwall, 160–2.

14. For a discussion of hybrid internalism, see Brink, 41. See also the discussion of non-constitutive existence internalism in Darwall, 158–61.

15. For discussion of the decision value framework, see Robert Nozick, *The Nature of Rationality* (Princeton: Princeton University Press, 1993), 41–63.

2

The Components of a Contractarian Argument for Preferring Justice

To justify the sense of justice to individuals, we shall argue that hypothetical contractors occupying a hypothetical choice situation would make a hypothetical choice to develop such a disposition.

Such a choice, as we shall understand it, has a purely heuristic function, revealing what members of our audience have the most reason to choose.[1] For an appeal to hypothetical choice to be capable of disalienating such individuals from the sense of justice, it must satisfy two conditions.

First, it must involve contractors who resemble us, who are situated similarly to us, and who operate with a conception of rationality to which we have some allegiance. Otherwise, such an appeal would not provide us reasons to maintain the sense of justice we each recognize as such from within our own perspective.

And second, it must involve contractors, a choice situation, and a conception of rationality specified independently of the domain of concepts associated with the sense of justice. Otherwise, such an appeal would not constitute a fundamental justification of this disposition.

In this chapter, we describe the components of a contractarian argument for the rationality of the sense of justice which satisfies both of these conditions.

Contractors

Our hypothetical contractors resemble us in each of the following ways.

Conceptions of the Good

Each has a set of preferences ranking the possible outcomes of her actions according to her reflective evaluation of these outcomes. Further, the preference set of each satisfies the formal conditions for defining an interval measure of preference .[2] Let a *conception of the good*, be just such a preference set.

Preference, so conceived, is consistent with a wide variety of contents. We could describe conceptions of the good in more determinate terms, as composed of objectively definable interests, for instance. But the less determinate our notion of a conception of the good, the more ways of life we can capture via this notion. Thus, by describing conceptions of the good as we have, we serve our goal of justifying the sense of justice as widely as possible within our pluralistic community.

Although this explains why we should describe contractors as possessing preferences, it does not explain why we should describe them as possessing coherent preferences. But an agent must possess coherent preferences for the question of the rationality of her choices to arise, at least on an instrumental theory of rationality. We describe contractors as preference-coherent so that we can invoke instrumentalism, the theory of rationality we shall defend as most appropriate for our purposes.

By describing contractors as preference-coherent, we differentiate them from ourselves. And one might think that in the face of this difference, we should deny that their choices can reveal what we have reason to do. But some of us have coherent preferences. And even those of us whose preferences are not fully coherent typically aspire to conducting ourselves in an instrumentally rational manner, at least within the context of social cooperation. But, since coherent preferences are a prerequisite of instrumentally rational conduct to aspire to instrumentally rational conduct is to aspire to having coherent preferences. Thus, having or aspiring to have coherent preferences, most of us have no grounds for denying that the choices of preference-coherent contractors can reveal what we have reason to do.

Limitations

Our contractors suffer from several limitations. First, they suffer from perceptual failings. They may overlook or mistake crucial features of their circumstances. Second, they have mnemonic limitations. Contractors have only a limited ability to assimilate, store, and recall information. Third, they suffer from cognitive failings. They may miscalculate the payoffs associated with their available alternatives. And finally, they suffer from psychological distortions: wishful thinking, feelings of paranoia, feelings of inferiority, and the like.

To varying degrees, we suffer from such limitations. Further, that this is so has a profound effect on our expectations of realizing our respective conceptions of the good. Hence, by building perceptual, mnemonic, cognitive, and psychological flaws into our contractors, we render them a more accurate representation of ourselves than they would otherwise be. And the more accurately contractors represent us, the more likely their choices are to reveal reasons for maintaining the sense of justice we each recognize as such.

Shallow Rationality

Our contractors suffer from flaws which may affect the accuracy of their perceptions, beliefs, and calculations. As a result, they may not always act rationally. Nonetheless, they always seek to act rationally. Thus, our contractors are ideally rational in the sense that they suffer from no motivational lapses, although not in the sense of being flawless reasoners.

But we can distinguish further among agents who are ideally rational in this sense. Let an agent be *deeply rational* if she always seeks to act rationally, and her intrinsic preferences respond directly, spontaneously, and automatically to rational criticism. And let an agent be *shallowly rational* if she always seeks to act rationally, but her intrinsic preferences do not so respond to rational criticism.

We characterize contractors as shallowly rational for two reasons. First, their limitations would prevent the mere promise of pragmatic benefit from causing a direct, spontaneous, and automatic change in their intrinsic preferences at least some of the time. Second, whether we are deeply rational, or capable of becoming so, is a controversial matter. And while we can generalize the conclusion that shallowly rational contractors would transform themselves to deeply rational contractors, the reverse is not true.[3]

One might think that shallowly rational agents are not ideally rational, and thus, of no normative significance, because they sometimes fail to prefer what there is most reason to prefer. But there is ample precedent for classifying shallow rationality as a species of ideal rationality. On a Humean conception of rationality, preference formation and choice are distinct, and only the latter is subject to rational appraisal. On such a conception, to be ideally rational just is to be shallowly rational. Thus, unless we are prepared to deny the possibility of Humean conceptions of ideal rationality, we cannot dismiss shallow rationality so easily.

One might accept shallow rationality as a species of ideal rationality, yet deny that we should characterize contractors as ideally rational in even this sense. For most of us are not ideally rational in any sense. And other things being equal, we should construct contractors to represent us more rather than less accurately, that their choices might reveal as clearly as possible what we have reason to do.

Sometimes, however, we serve our project better by suppressing or exaggerating features of ourselves in constructing contractors than by representing ourselves faithfully. By characterizing contractors as ideally rational, for instance, we render their choices more tractable to analysis. Such useful distortions are permissible so long as they do not prevent the choices of contractors from revealing reasons for maintaining the sense of justice we recognize as such.

And our characterization of contractors as ideally rational falls into this class of distortions. For ideally rational contractors do not exhibit some trait that we lack entirely. Rather, they exhibit a trait of ours, a commitment to acting rationally, more consistently than we ourselves do. And though we are not ideally rational, we typically aspire to approach this ideal as closely as we can, at least within the context of social cooperation. Viewing ideally rational contractors as amplifications of ourselves worth emulating, we must recognize their choices as revealing what we ourselves have reason to do.

Nontuism

Our contractors are *nontuistic*, taking no interest in whether the preferences of their fellows are satisfied. With respect to other contractors, they are neither benevolent nor malevolent.

Were contractors *tuistic*, each would assess actions not just in terms of her own expectations, but also in terms of the expectations of others. And if contractors did so, keeping track of the satisfaction of their preferences would be a daunting task. We assume nontuism so as to simplify this task.

The diverse and complex interests we take in one another's interests are morally significant.[4] And it is no virtue of a moral argument that it abstracts away significant aspects of our moral lives for the sake of simplicity. But we seek to justify the sense of justice to individuals *qua* members of a scheme of social cooperation like our own. And among us, social cooperation involves many, many individuals, most of whom remain anonymous to one another. Within this context, individuals may concern themselves with the preferences of those they love or hate. Typically, however, they do not care about the preferences of those they regard as no more than fellow participants of social cooperation. Hence, nontuism describes the preferences of most of us accurately in the context where the sense of justice finds expression. Thus, the nontuism of contractors affords most of us no grounds for rejecting them as representations of ourselves.

Even if this is true in general, there are some who care one way or the other about the interests of all of those with whom we cooperate. *Benevolent* individuals prefer that the preferences of their fellow cooperators be satisfied. *Malevolent* individuals prefer that the preferences of their fellow cooperators be frustrated.

For all but the most malevolent members of our audience, however, an appeal to their tuistic preferences would not undermine our justification of the sense of justice. Those who prefer that the preferences of all of their fellows be satisfied have more reason than what an appeal to their non-tuistic preferences would reveal to maintain the sense of justice. The same is true of those who prefer that the preferences of only certain of their fellows be satisfied, at least where the expectations of individuals overlap in ways that cannot always be ascertained prior to action.[5] And those with a mix of benevolent and malevolent preferences who would realize no less utility from satisfying the former than the latter have no less reason to maintain the sense of justice than an appeal to their nontuistic preferences alone would reveal. Thus, no one exhibiting tuistic preferences in any of the above configurations has any less reason to maintain the sense of justice than one of our nontuistic contractors.

But if an individual would realize more utility from satisfying her malevolent preferences than from satisfying her other preferences, she would have less reason to maintain the sense of justice than one of our contractors. Indeed, reason would recommend against such individuals maintaining the sense of justice.

This indicates a limitation of our justification of the sense of justice. Some malevolent members of our audience may have less to gain from treating others justly than from treating them unjustly. And by appealing to the preferences of such individuals, we cannot reveal what they recognize as sufficient reason to maintain the sense of justice. We shall discuss the implications of this limitation, and our prospects for overcoming it, in the final chapter of this book.

Were all of us predominantly malevolent, our project could not succeed. For in this case, by treating others justly, we would preclude the maximal satisfaction of our own preferences. And where it is not rational to act justly rather than unjustly, it is not rational to maintain the disposition to do so.[6] But since we are not all predominantly malevolent, we should not be dismayed by our inability to justify this disposition to individuals who are all so.

Opacity

Our contractors are *opaque* to one another, unable to determine one another's dispositions with a probability greater than chance before interacting with one another. They cannot read one another's dispositions from one another's appearance, demeanor, gestures, word choices, inflections, or the like.

We might have characterized contractors as *transparent*, able to determine one another's dispositions with certainty. But had we done so, there would be no question about the rationality of their maintaining the sense of justice. For each would be able to engage others in cooperation only if she maintained such a disposition.

Or we might have characterized contractors as *translucent*, able to determine one another's dispositions with a probability somewhat greater than chance. But by assuming translucency rather than opacity, we would provide just contractors the option of refusing to cooperate with those they identify as bad cooperative risks, decreasing the opportunities for unjust contractors to interact with others. And by so doing, we would advantage just over unjust contractors.

These considerations imply that while we can generalize an argument for the rationality of maintaining the sense of justice from opacity to either transparency or translucency, the reverse is not true. Since there is considerable disagreement about just where along the continuum between transparency and opacity we find ourselves, we serve our project best by characterizing contractors as opaque.[7]

No Sense of Justice

Finally, when they begin deliberating, our contractors lack the sense of justice. Were we to show that contractors exhibiting the sense of justice would choose to maintain it, we could not be certain that some of their reasons for so choosing did not derive from this disposition itself, spoiling our attempt at fundamental justification.

Most of us exhibit the sense of justice to some degree or another, but this will not preclude the choices of contractors who lack such a disposition from revealing what we have reason to do. To exhibit the sense of justice is to value acting justly rather than unjustly for its own sake. But valuing just over unjust actions intrinsically, an agent has a reason to affirm any disposition she expects to cause her to act justly rather than unjustly. Thus, those of us who exhibit the sense of justice have reasons beyond those revealed by the choices of our contractors for maintaining this disposition.

A Choice Situation

Having described our contractors, we turn to constructing their choice situation.

Agreement on a Conception of Justice

In this choice situation, contractors are agreed upon a particular conception of justice. That is, even though they do not agree that they ought to internalize a disposition to act justly rather than unjustly, they agree about what justice is. Perhaps they have inherited their conception of justice, or perhaps they have chosen it. For our purposes, it does not matter. Nor does its content. But whatever this content, contractors regard it as fixed, so that they are choosing only whether and how to implement it.[8]

By representing contractors as agreed upon some unspecified conception of justice, we exclude appeals to particular conceptions from their choice situation. Only by so doing can we insure that our justification of the sense of justice will be fundamental, and that it will remain so in the face of changes to our conception of justice.

One might think that rationality requires contractors to adopt a particular conception of justice. And if appeals to a particular conception of justice could be reduced to appeals to rationality, we would not need to exclude such conceptions from contractors' choice situation, for they would not compromise our fundamental justification of the sense of justice. Appealing to these considerations, one might argue that we should represent contractors as agreed upon the conception of justice rationality requires them to adopt.

The relationship between rationality and the content of justice is a matter of controversy. Some who maintain that rationality recommends a particular conception of justice to us disagree about its recommendations.[9] Others deny that rationality recommends any particular conception of justice to us.[10] But we can justify the sense of justice to members of our audience without defending the rationality of any particular conception of justice. And by refusing to link our justification of the sense of justice to any particular conception of justice, we avoid saddling it with a controversial and unnecessary premise.[11]

One might worry that this liberality will get us into trouble. For there are conceptions of justice the adoption of which would preclude individuals from developing the sense of justice. Consider, for example, a conception which forbids individuals to act justly rather than unjustly because they value doing so for its own sake. Because we do not specify the conception of justice upon which contractors are agreed, we leave open the possibility that they are agreed upon a conception which would preclude them from developing the sense of justice. And were contractors agreed upon such a conception, developing the sense of justice would not be rational for them, and an appeal to their choices could not rationalize the sense of justice to us.

This possibility limits the scope of our conclusions, forcing us to acknowledge that our justification of the sense of justice is not compatible with all possible conceptions of justice. But since we are not governed by a conception which precludes us from developing the sense of justice, this does not hinder our attempt to provide members of our community with a fundamental justification of the sense of justice.

In the face of our own disagreements about justice, one might worry that the choices of contractors who agree about justice can reveal nothing about what we have reason to do. But there is a core conception of justice upon which virtually all of us agree, a conception including, at the very least, some of the rights articulated in the U. S. Constitution. We govern ourselves with this conception, passing laws to further it, appealing to these laws to resolve our disputes, and punishing those who violate these laws. Thus, contractors differ from us not in agreeing upon a conception of justice, but in the extent of the conception upon which they agree. And an appeal to the choices of such contractors can reveal reasons for us to internalize the conception upon which we do agree.

Structure of This Choice Situation

Let a *strategy* be a sequence of choices. Let an *individual strategy* be a sequence of choices made by one agent. To choose an individual strategy, an agent decides how she shall choose in a sequence of choices. To implement an individual strategy, an agent chooses sequentially as it specifies. Let a *joint strategy* be a sequence of choices requiring two or more agents to coordinate their individual strategies. To choose a joint strategy, a group of agents agrees upon how each shall choose in a sequence of choices. To implement a joint strategy, each chooses sequentially as it specifies.

Given these distinctions, we can describe the structure of the choice situation occupied by contractors. It involves two discreet stages. At the first stage, contractors agree upon a joint strategy for implementing rules of justice, and take whatever measures are required to insure that they can execute this strategy successfully. At the second stage, they choose individual strategies for satisfying their preferences within the context created by their actions at the first stage. As we shall conceive of this choice situation, contractors can reach its second stage only by completing the tasks comprising its first stage.

Settling upon a feasible joint strategy for putting rules of justice into practice is distinct from choosing an individual strategy for maximizing under a set of such rules. And each of these tasks involves its own distinctive problems. By dividing contractors' choice situation into discreet stages, we isolate the problems involved in each of these tasks, the better to solve them.

Moreover, we each must choose whether or not to maintain the sense of justice in a community where a joint strategy for implementing rules of justice has already been settled upon, and the measures required to insure that we can execute this strategy successfully have already been taken. By dividing contractors' choice situation as we have, we insure that contractors must choose whether or not to maintain the sense of justice under similar conditions, rendering it a more accurate representation of our circumstances than it would otherwise be.

What Contractors Know

Within their choice situation, contractors have available most of the same information about themselves and the world that we do.

They know that they occupy the circumstances of justice.[12]

They know that they are agreed upon a conception of justice and, they know its content.

Except when we note otherwise, they have access to all of the techniques, data, explanations, and predictions supplied us by the natural and social sciences. And we are to imagine this information being updated if and when we make advances bearing on the rationality of maintaining the sense of justice.

Each knows her own personal and social characteristics. Personal characteristics include intelligence, gender, aptitudes, handicaps, strength, appearance, and the like. Examples of social characteristics are social standing, economic standing, occupation, membership in various groups, and so on.

Further, this knowledge involves a comparative component. Knowing her intelligence, a contractor knows how she compares with her fellows along the dimension of intelligence. Knowing her economic standing, a contractor knows how she compares with her fellows along the dimensions of income and wealth. And the same goes for what contractors know of their other personal and social characteristics.

Finally, each knows the preferences comprising her own conception of the good. Confronted with any two possible outcomes of an action, she can rank these outcomes relative to one another, and she can associate cardinal utility payoffs with each of them.

We allow contractors all of this information because it corresponds to information available to us. Insofar as contractors have access to the same sorts of information as we do, conditions within their choice situation mirror conditions within our own community.

One might worry, however, about our willingness to update the information available to our contractors. For by revising our argument for the rationality of the sense of justice to reflect significant developments in the natural and social sciences, we might invalidate it. For our purposes, however, such developments count as significant only if they bear upon how rational individuals ought to implement rules of justice, or how they ought to negotiate living under such rules. Were a technology invented rendering individuals transparent to one another, for instance, we should have to rethink our conclusions. And we should have to do the same if we discovered that all human limitations could be completely remedied. But history indicates that such dramatic developments are not commonplace. And in the event of any such development, we would be well advised to rethink the relationship between rationality and the sense of justice.

One might also worry that by providing contractors all of the information supplied us by the natural and social sciences, we risk alienating some of our audience. After all, some of this information is controversial. But because contractors resemble us in their differing personal characteristics, social characteristics, and preferences, what is controversial among us will be controversial among them. And in the course of their deliberations, contractors could successfully appeal only to uncontroversial information. Thus, controversial information will do no work in our justification of the sense of justice. And the mere availability of such information to contractors provides us no reason for rejecting them as representations of ourselves, for similar information is available to us.

What Contractors Do Not Know

There are two sorts of information to which contractors do not have access. First, although each knows her own conception of the good, none knows others' conceptions of the good. Second, while each knows that she suffers from perceptual, mnemonic, cognitive, and psychological limitations, none knows the extent of her limitations.

Conceptions of the good, as we have analyzed them, are comprised of preferences. And preferences, as we shall analyze them, are dispositions to choose. Thus, that contractors do not know others' conceptions of the good follows from our characterization of them as opaque.

One might worry that contractors who do no know others' conceptions of the good fail to represent us accurately, since most of us know the preferences of at least some of our fellows. We do not, however, typically know the conceptions of the good of those we view as no more than fellow participants in social cooperation. Thus, by denying contractors knowledge of their fellows' conceptions of the good, we approximate our circumstances, at least *qua* participants in such a scheme.

Even if we do not know most others' conceptions of the good, one might argue, we surely know the extent of our own limitations. We encounter these daily, after all, and at very close range. But the very nature of our limitations insures that we have little reliable information about them. Our perceptual, cognitive, and mnemonic limitations make it difficult for each us to perceive, determine, and recall just what our particular limitations are. This difficulty is compounded by psychological distortions causing us to misrepresent the extent of our limitations to ourselves, inferiority and superiority complexes, for instance. And it is further compounded by the existence of psychological distortions like wishful thinking or paranoia which, by their very nature, are opaque to those of us afflicted by them.

Still, we can learn something about the extent of our limitations by observing ourselves over time. Thus, by assuming that contractors know nothing of their limitations, we exaggerate our own plight somewhat. In doing so, however, we introduce an element of uncertainty into contractors' choice situation, uncertainty on the part of each about the outcome of her decisions. And such uncertainty permeates our own lives, especially when we are making choices with possible effects in the distant future, as when we choose whether or not to maintain the sense of justice. Hence, by assuming that contractors know nothing about the extent of their limitations, we mirror the sort of uncertainty which figures so prominently in our own lives.

Rationality

To show that within the above choice situation, contractors would choose to develop and maintain the sense of justice, we must appeal to a conception of rationality. In describing this conception, the distinction between a theory of rationality and a decision rule is helpful.[13]

A theory of rationality specifies a determinate goal for action in abstract terms. A decision rule tells individuals how to realize the goal specified by a theory of rationality. It provides individuals with guidance in the particulars of achieving rational success. In developing a fundamental justification of the sense of justice, we shall appeal to a theory of rationality, and to several decision rules associated with it.

Instrumental Rationality

So far as a theory of rationality goes, we shall appeal to instrumentalism, defining substantive rationality in terms of choosing efficient means to one's ends. This appeal, conjoined with our representation of ends in terms of coherent preferences, yields an objective criterion of rational success.[14] Rational choice is choice which maximizes utility, where utility is a measure of the satisfaction of the preferences we have described.

One might object to instrumentalism on pragmatic grounds. There are times when the costs of calculating the most effective means to one's ends outweigh the benefits of doing so. Other times, weighing the costs and benefits of one's alternatives changes the nature of these alternatives for the worse.[15] And at still other times, reasoning in a straightforwardly instrumental manner precludes one from capitalizing fully on beneficial opportunities.[16] Drawing upon an argument that such cases are commonplace, one might argue that we would do better at realizing our ends were we not instrumental reasoners, and that for this reason, we ought to reject instrumentalism.

But this objection ignores the distinction between a theory of rationality and a decision rule. We have assumed that rational choice maximizes utility. But we have not assumed that to choose rationally, individuals must follow a decision rule which is isomorphic with the injunction to maximize utility. In fact, when individuals would do better at realizing their ends by following some other rule, instrumental rationality instructs them to do so. And so, that individuals would do better at achieving their ends in some contexts by disregarding the injunction to maximize is no objection to instrumentalism.

We appeal to instrumentalism for three reasons.

First, instrumentalism is consistent with a wide variety of conceptions of the good. Instrumentalism does not discriminate among preferences according to their appropriateness for guiding action. If a set of preferences is coherent, then instrumentalism treats it as a valid basis for action. This suits it to grounding an argument that individuals with diverse conceptions of the good ought to maintain the sense of justice.

Second, although philosophically-inclined individuals disagree about the nature of rationality, there is a core of agreement among them. For every proposed theory of rationality aspiring to completeness includes instrumentalism within it.[17] And of the major extant theories of rationality, only instrumentalism enjoys this distinction. There is, thus, something like a consensus among philosophically-inclined individuals that instrumentalism constitutes (at least) part of rationality.

As an alternative to instrumentalism, one might identify rationality with acting upon the balance of whatever reasons one has to act. An appeal to this theory of rationality could generate a fundamental justification of the sense of justice only if one excluded from the balance of reasons all reasons deriving from the sense of justice. But even given this restriction, this theory appears to be weaker than instrumentalism, at least in the sense of excluding fewer substantive accounts of rationality. And being weaker than instrumentalism, one might think it would be less contentious.[18]

But while this theory is consistent with more substantive theories of rationality than instrumentalism, it does not itself constitute such a theory, at least not absent an account of what counts as a reason for action. For absent such an account, we cannot appeal to this theory to rule out any actions at all as irrational. Thus, by itself, this theory does not specify a determinate goal for action, not even in the abstract.

If we conjoin it to the claim that only an agent's preferences provide her with reasons for action, this theory of rationality reduces to instrumentalism. And if we conjoin it to some other account of reasons for action which enjoys fairly broad support within our community, then presumably we will end up with one of instrumentalism's major competitors. But these, we have already noticed, are each more contentious than instrumentalism.

We might leave it to individuals to determine what counts as a reason for action, claiming that rationality requires each to act upon the balance of those considerations she considers to be reasons for action. But to do so is to assert a conceptual link between what an agent considers rational for her and what is rational for her. And to assert such a link is to contradict the theories of rationality dominant within our own community. For although these theories define rationality differently, all agree that an agent can do what she considers rational without acting rationally. Since instrumentalism does not contradict any of our dominant theories of rationality, being contained within each of them as a part, it is less contentious than the proposal we have been considering.

And third, instrumentalism provides individuals with reasons for maintaining the sense of justice which do not derive from this disposition. And we can provide individuals with a fundamental justification of the sense of justice only by appealing to such reasons.

One might yet worry about instrumentalism's capacity for providing individuals with reasons for maintaining the sense of justice. Distinguishing between rational preferences and mere whims, one might argue that appeals to rational preferences reveal reasons for action, while appeals to mere whims do not.[19] And were this so, then we could show that maintaining the sense of justice would maximize over an agent's preferences without providing her with any reason to do so.

This worry assumes a different analysis of preference than we assume. On this worry, preference is not a primitive attitude of evaluation which survives reflection. Rather, it is, or is informed by, a judgement about value. As such, it is sustained by reason, and open to rational criticism. But we avoid this analysis of preference for a reason. It presupposes a conception of rationality with more content than instrumentalism, one that rules out some preferences as irrational. But philosophically-inclined individuals do not agree upon any such conception of rationality.[20] Thus, if we wish to justify the sense of justice to such individuals, we should avoid appealing to one. Absent such an appeal, however, rational preferences and mere whims cannot be distinguished, and the above objection cannot be sustained.[21]

Present-Aim Instrumentalism

There are three variants of instrumentalism. *Present-aim rationality* enjoins the satisfaction of present preferences only. *Prudence* enjoins the satisfaction of present and future preferences.[22] And *atemporal rationality* enjoins the satisfaction of past, present, and future preferences.[23]

We appeal to present-aim rationality rather than prudence or atemporal rationality for two reasons.

First, all variants of instrumentalism agree that appeals to present preferences reveal reasons for action to individuals. Not all, however, agree that appeals to past and future preferences do so. And in the face of this disagreement, only an appeal to present-aim rationality can reveal to all with a commitment to instrumental rationality reasons they recognize for maintaining the sense of justice.

And second, in conjunction with our contractors and their choice situation, only an appeal to present-aim rationality can yield a fundamental justification of the sense of justice. Since our contractors have no sense of justice, an argument that present-aim rationality requires them to develop such a disposition will reveal only reasons for doing so which do not derive from the sense of justice itself. Both prudence and atemporal rationality, however, require our contractors to consider the utility they might realize from satisfying future preferences in choosing whether or not to develop the sense of justice. One preference each might acquire is an intrinsic preference for acting justly rather than unjustly, the sense of justice. And if contractors had to consider the utility they might realize from satisfying such a preference in choosing whether or not to develop one, an appeal to their choices would not yield a fundamental justification of the sense of justice.

Were we to bracket any preferences contractors might acquire for acting justly rather than unjustly, an analysis of their choices in terms of prudence or atemporal rationality could, in principle, yield a fundamental justification of the sense of justice. But to do so would be to handicap just contractors too much in their maximizing efforts. For were we to bracket the utility just contractors would realize from their most-preferred outcomes without bracketing the utility unjust contractors would realize from their most-preferred outcomes, being just could hardly fail to pay contractors less than being unjust. Since just members of our own community operate under no such handicap, however, this result would indicate nothing about the rationality or irrationality of our maintaining the sense of justice.

Decision Rules for Instrumentally Rational Agents

When an agent knows the outcomes of her actions with certainty, maximizing over her preferences is unproblematic.

Under conditions of *risk*, when an agent knows only the probabilities associated with the possible outcomes of her actions, doing so is more difficult. There is, however, a broad consensus that under risk, instrumentally rational agents ought to maximize expected utility.[24]

Under conditions of *uncertainty*, when agents cannot determine the probabilities associated with the possible outcomes of their actions, no such consensus exists. Since their choice situation involves considerable uncertainty, determining whether or not contractors would choose to become just requires us to say something about how instrumentally rational agents ought to choose under uncertainty.

A Short List of Decision Rules.   There may be no single decision rule adherence to which would maximize utility under uncertainty. And even if one such rule exists, any attempt to isolate it would be controversial. For these reasons, we shall not justify the sense of justice by appealing to any single decision rule for choice under uncertainty. Instead, we shall generate a short list of such rules, and argue that contractors would choose to become just by appealing to the rules on this list.

This way of proceeding is less than ideal, for it requires us to conditionalize our conclusions on the adequacy of the short list from which we begin. But by so proceeding, we can reduce the problem of determining whether contractors would choose to become just to manageable proportions. And besides, we can always update our argument for the rationality of the sense of justice by expanding this short list, if and when new and more plausible decision rules become available.

First on our short list is the maximin rule, which instructs agents to choose that option, from among those available, with the best worst possible outcome. Among philosophically-inclined individuals, maximin is among the most favored decision rules for choice under uncertainty. By including it on our short list, we block the objection that we have loaded this list with obscure decision rules designed expressly to generate our desired results.

Second on our short list is Gregory S. Kavka's disaster avoidance principle, which instructs agents to choose that option, from among those available, which minimizes the probability of any disastrous outcome occurring.[25] This decision rule is neither widely known nor widely accepted. Nonetheless, we include it on our short list because it was designed for contexts exhibiting considerable uncertainty and the potential for disaster, and contractors' choice situation is such a context.

We round our short list out with the expected utility principle, which instructs agents to choose that action, from among those available, which maximizes expected utility. On the dominant view of rationality within our community, we ought to follow this rule under risk. The more uncertainty a choice situation involves, however, the less support the expected utility principle enjoys among philosophically-inclined individuals. Nonetheless, we include this rule on our short list because many think that it should regulate choice under risk and limited uncertainty, and some regard it as our best hope for maximizing under complete uncertainty.

Notable Omissions.   There are a few other decision rules which might seem like obvious candidates for our short list. And to defend this list, we must justify not only its contents, but also its most notable omissions.

Our short list includes only *direct* decision rules, rules which never require agents to choose against the balance of their preferences. But one might think that given recent interest in *indirect* decision rules, rules which sometimes require agents to choose against the balance of their preferences, it should include at least one such rule as well.

On instrumentalism, an agent chooses rationally unless her chosen option yields her less utility than choosing one of her other available options would have yielded her. Rationality, so conceived, requires an agent to adopt an indirect decision rule only when her doing so would create a situation in which she would realize more utility by violating this rule than by following it. But having managed to create such a situation, such an agent would realize more utility by violating whatever indirect decision rule she has adopted than by following it.[26] Thus, any time it is rational for an agent to adopt an indirect decision rule, it will be irrational for her to do as this rule requires. And thus, facing any given choice, it is either irrational for an agent to adopt an indirect decision rule, or irrational for her to follow any such rule rationality requires her to adopt. And so, we omit indirect decision rules from our short list because rationality, as we have characterized it, precludes agents from adopting and following such rules.

One might worry that instrumentalism also precludes agents from choosing according to the maximin rule, the disaster avoidance principle, and the expected utility principle. For under risk or uncertainty, following any of these rules might yield an agent less than maximal utility. But from an instrumentalist perspective, the problem with indirect decision rules is not that by following one, an agent might fail to maximize utility. After all, under risk or uncertainty, this is a possible outcome of following any decision rule. Rather, it is that an agent cannot adopt and follow an indirect decision rule without acting irrationally. The conception of rationality we have assumed is forgiving, but not so forgiving as to permit agents to operate with such rules.

Also notably absent from our short list is any sort of satisficing decision rule. Such rules require agents to choose the first action from among their available alternatives involving a satisfactory utility payoff. There exist situations in which an agent can only maximize her global utility by ceasing to seek a local optimum.[27] Indeed, the choice of whether or not to maintain the sense of justice may be such a situation. So why not expand our short list to include a satisficing rule?

When an agent knows all of the outcomes of her available actions with certainty, she satisfices by choosing the first involving a satisfactory utility payoff. Under conditions of risk, it is less clear what satisficing entails. But this could be clarified. We might, for instance, require agents to choose the first available alternative involving a satisfactory expected utility. Under conditions of uncertainty, however, it is not at all clear what satisficing entails. Are agents to choose the first action one possible outcome of which involves a satisfactory payoff? The first action most of the possible outcomes of which involve such a payoff? The first action all of the possible outcomes of which involve such a payoff? None of the obvious adaptations of the satisficing rule to conditions of uncertainty enjoy any support among us as decision rules for choosing under uncertainty. Thus, we have nothing to gain by including any of these on our short list of such rules.

A Framework for Adjudicating Between Decision Rules.   As it turns out, the three decision rules on our short list do not agree in their recommendations to contractors. Thus, if we wish to appeal to this list to determine whether or not contractors would choose to become just, we require some method of adjudicating among the competing recommendations of different decision rules.

The *decision value framework,* developed by Robert Nozick, provides us with one such method.[28] An agent might have some confidence in each of two decision rules which place competing demands on her, say the causal and the evidential expected utility principles.[29] Let $W(c)$ be a measure of her confidence in the causal expected utility principle, and $W(e)$ be a measure of her confidence in the evidential expected utility principle. And let $CEU(A)$ be the causal expected utility of act A, and $EEU(A)$ be the evidential expected utility of act A. Then associated with each act A available to any such agent, there is a decision value (DV), an index measuring its combined, confidence-weighted causal and evidential expected utilities:

$$DV(A) = W(c) \times CEU(A) + W(e) \times EEU(A).$$

By requiring that agents maximize decision value, we adjudicate between the competing demands of the causal and the evidential expected utility principles upon any such agent.

We shall adapt the decision value framework to the task of adjudicating among the competing demands of the maximin, disaster avoidance, and expected utility principles upon instrumentally rational agents choosing under uncertainty. Let $W(m)$, $W(d)$, and $W(e)$ be the respective weights that an agent assigns to each of these principles. There are various restrictions we might impose upon the values of $W(m)$, $W(d)$, and

$W(e)$, but we shall require only that they be positive.[30] Let $UWO(A)$ be the utility associated with the worst outcome of act A, $PAD(A)$ be the probability of avoiding disaster if one performs act A, and $EU(A)$ be the expected utility of act A.[31] For each act, A, available to an agent, we define its decision value as follows:

$$DV(A) = W(m) \times UWO(A) + W(d) \times PAD(A) + W(e) \times EU(A)$$

So as to adjudicate among the maximin, disaster avoidance, and expected utility principles, we shall require agents to maximize decision value when choosing under uncertainty.

As it turns out, we need know very little about the values of $W(m)$, $W(d)$, and $W(e)$ to apply the decision value framework within contractors' choice situation. Nonetheless, we shall say something about how agents are to assign weights to the maximin, disaster avoidance, and expected utility principles, so as to block the objection that we have assigned values to $W(m)$, $W(d)$, and $W(e)$ arbitrarily.[32]

Different decision rules have been developed to guide choice in different contexts. An agent is apt to maximize utility by following a given rule if her choice situation resembles closely the context for which this rule was developed. And following a given rule is apt to fail to maximize utility for an agent if her choice situation bears little or no resemblance to the context for which this rule was developed.

But this suggests how agents might assign weights to the maximin, disaster avoidance, and expected utility principles.[33] Let them first identify the most important features of the contexts for which each of these rules was developed. These constitute the *plausibility conditions* for each of these rules, the conditions under which following each is a plausible means to maximizing utility. Then let each agent analyze her choice situation, and determine the extent to which it satisfies these plausibility conditions. If her choice situation satisfies few or none of the plausibility conditions for a given rule, and if the conditions it satisfies are unimportant, each should assign little or no weight to that rule. If her choice situation satisfies most or all of the plausibility conditions for a given rule, and if the conditions it satisfies are important, each should assign a significant positive weight to that rule.

Clearly, this procedure is radically underspecified. I have not explained, for instance, how agents are to handle cases in which a choice situation satisfies a middling number of the plausibility conditions for a rule. Nor have I indicated how agents are to determine the relative weight of two rules in a choice situation satisfying some of the plausibility conditions of each of them. Nor have I said anything about how agents are to get from "little or no weight" and "significant positive weight" to particular values for $W(m)$, $W(d)$, and $W(e)$. I shall, however, resist the temptation to provide any more details on how instrumentally rational agents might assign weights to competing decision rules under uncertainty. Any such details are sure to be controversial, and we do not require them to adjudicate between the rules on our short list, at least not within the choice situation we have defined.

The decision value framework, adapted as we have described, can accommodate the views of anyone believing that under uncertainty, instrumentally rational agents ought to choose according to one or more of the rules on our short list. And by adapting this framework further, we could accommodate more and different views on instrumentally rational choice under uncertainty, if ever we had to expand our short list of decision rules. Thus, the decision value framework is well-suited to representing instrumentally rational choice under uncertainty to an audience divided on the proper nature of such choice.

Conclusion

In this chapter, we have described the justification of the sense of justice we hope to develop, and we have outlined our methodology for developing it. As this methodology requires, we have constructed contractors and a choice situation, and delineated a conception of rationality to guide the choices of these contractors within this choice situation. Having described in detail the inputs of our contractarian argument for the rationality of the sense of justice, we turn to describing its output: self-transformation.

Notes

1. Here I follow Christopher Morris. See Christopher Morris, "Moral Standing and Rational-Choice Contractarianism," in *Contractarianism and Rational Choice*, ed. Peter Vallentyne (Cambridge: Cambridge University Press, 1991), 76–95.

2. These conditions are completeness, transitivity, monotonicity, substitutability, reduction of compound lotteries, and continuity. For a discussion of them, see R. D. Luce and H. Raiffa, *Games and Decisions* (New York: John Wiley & Sons, Inc., 1957), Chapter 2.

3. That contractors would transform themselves for a price implies that they would do so for free, but that contractors would transform themselves for free does not imply that they would do so for a price.

4. For a discussion of this point, see Morris, 129.

5. Rawls makes a similar point in arguing that possession of a sense of justice is a good for individuals. See John Rawls, *A Theory of Justice* (Cambridge: Harvard University Press, 1971), 570–1.

6. For a similar argument, see David Gauthier, "Morality, Rational Choice, and Semantic Representation," *Social Philosophy and Policy* 5 (1988): 214.

7. For a discussion of the debate among philosophically-inclined members of our community about translucency, see Chapter 3.

8. Does so characterizing contractors preclude us from justifying a sense of justice to Marxists, and to others whose conception of justice varies over epochs? No, for a Marxist sense of justice would track the content of the Marxist conception of justice, so that its urgings would vary over epochs as well.

9. See, for instance, the different conceptions of justice rationalized in David Gauthier, *Morals by Agreement* (New York: Oxford University Press, 1986), Gregory S. Kavka, *Hobbesian Moral and Political Theory* (Princeton: Princeton University Press, 1986), and Jan Narveson, *The Libertarian Idea* (Philadelphia: Temple University Press, 1988).

10. See, for instance, Robert Sugden, "Contractarianism and Norms," *Ethics* 100 (1990): 768–86.

11. By setting to one side the question of how rationality is related to the content of justice, I do not mean to imply that this question is uninteresting or insignificant. But for all the reasons we have discussed, providing individuals with a fundamental justification of the sense of justice is important whatever the relationship between rationality and the content of justice turns out to be.

12. For a discussion of the circumstances of justice, see Chapter 1.

13. Many have made similar distinctions. See, for example, Peter Danielson, *Artificial Morality* (New York: Routledge, 1992), 62.

14. For a detailed treatment of how utility maximization can be derived from the characterization of rationality as efficient choice over coherent preferences, see David Gauthier, "Reason and Maximization," *Canadian Journal of Philosophy* 4 (1975): 411–33.

15. This can happen when, for instance, one's highest ranked outcome requires one to act spontaneously. For a discussion of such situations, see David Schmidtz, *Rational Choice and Moral Agency* (Princeton: Princeton University Press, 1995), 21.

16. For a discussion of one such case, the Prisoner's Dilemma, see Richmond Campbell, "Background for the Uninitiated," in *Paradoxes of Rationality and Cooperation*, ed. Richmond Campbell and Lanning Sowden (Vancouver: University of British Columbia Press, 1985), 3–41. For a discussion of another, Newcomb's Problem, see David Gauthier, "In the Neighborhood of the Newcomb-Predictor," *Proceedings of The Aristotelian Society* 89 (1988–89): 179–94. For a less contrived case, see Derek Parfit, *Reasons and Persons* (Oxford: Oxford University Press, 1984), 7.

17. For a similar point, see Robert Nozick, *The Nature of Rationality* (Princeton: Princeton University Press, 1993), 133. See also Schmidtz, 4.

18. I thank Christopher Morris for this objection.

19. For accounts that distinguish in this manner among preferences, see David O. Brink, *Moral Realism and the Foundations of Ethics* (New York: Cornell University Press, 1989), 63–6, Stephen L. Darwall, *Impartial Reason* (London: Cornell University Press, 1983), 85–100, and Thomas Nagel, *The Possibility of Altruism* (Oxford: Oxford University Press, 1970), 27–56.

20. For differing accounts of the requirements that rationality imposes on preferences, see Richard Brandt, *A Theory of the Good and the Right* (Oxford: Clarendon Press, 1979), 110–29, Brink, 62–6, Darwall, 85–100, and Nozick, 139–51.

21. But this does not imply that everything we call a "whim" in ordinary language belongs in an agent's preference set. If a given "whim" corresponds to one of an agent's reflective evaluative attitudes, then it belongs in her preference set. If it does not, then it is not one of her preferences.

22. For a discussion of one such account, see Duncan MacIntosh, "Persons and the Satisfaction of Preferences: Problems in the Rational Kinematics of Values," *The Journal of Philosophy* 90 (1993): 163–80.

23. See, for instance, the account of prudence in Nagel, 27–76, and the discussion of the Self-interest Theory in Parfit, 149–86.

24. To maximize expected utility, an agent sums the products of the probabilities and utilities associated with each possible outcome of each action available to her, and then chooses the available action involving the highest such sum.

25. See Gregory S. Kavka, "Deterrence, Utility, and Rational Choice," *Theory and Decision* 12 (1980): 41–60.

26. For a similar point, see Duncan MacIntosh, "Preference's Progress: Rational Self-Alteration and the Rationality of Morality," *Dialogue* 30 (1991): 22.

27. For examples of some such situations, see Schmidtz, 28–45.

28. See Nozick, 41–63.

29. As Robert Nozick describes it, evidential expected utility theory specifies that the utilities of the possible outcomes of an action be weighted by their conditional probabilities given these actions. Causal expected utility theory specifies that these utilities be weighted by some causal-probabilistic relation indicating direct causal influence. See Nozick, 43.

30. By so specifying the values of $W(m)$, $W(d)$, and $W(e)$, we leave the interpretation of these terms open. They could be measures of a chooser's perception of the legitimate force of maximin, disaster avoidance, and expected utility reasoning within a particular choice situation, in which case they might sum to anything at all. Or they could be the chooser's estimates of the probability that each of these rules is the best rule to guide a particular choice, in which case they must sum to one. For our purposes, it does not matter.

31. In integrating the disaster avoidance principle into the decision value framework, I am utilizing suggestions Gregory S. Kavka makes in developing a version of the disaster avoidance principle which exhibits transitivity. See Kavka, "Deterrence," 53–4.

32. Robert Nozick is of little help here: "I would welcome a theory to specify or restrict the weights . . ." See Nozick, 46.

33. That decision rules are differentially plausible in different contexts, that we can determine the plausibility conditions for different rules, and that we can argue for the appropriateness of particular rules in particular contexts by appealing to such conditions, have been suggested by several individuals. See, for example, Rawls, 154–5, and Kavka, "Deterrence," 50–1.

3

Self-Transformation

We shall argue that maximizing decision value within their choice situation, our contractors would choose to transform themselves into just individuals. Such self-transformation, as we shall conceive of it, involves contractors altering their own preferences. Thus, a discussion of self-transformation must begin with a discussion of preference, and the related notion of utility.

Preference, Utility, and Preference Orderings

Preference is a two-place relation between states of affairs conceived of as the possible outcomes of actions. Rational choice theory does not analyze particular relations of preference, which are taken as given, but sets of such relations attributed to individual agents.

More specifically, it analyzes sets of preferences which are coherent. Traditionally, a *coherent* preference set is one which is both complete and transitive.[1] An agent's preference set is *complete* if, given any two of its members, she either prefers one to the other or is indifferent between them. That a preference set is *transitive* implies: 1) for any members X, Y, and Z, if an agent prefers X to Y and Y to Z, then she also prefers X to Z, and 2) for any members X, Y, and Z, if an agent is indifferent between X and Y and between Y and Z, then she is also indifferent between X and Z.

Utility is a measure of preference. More specifically, it is a measure of the value of the outcomes ranked by an agent's preferences. We assign utility to the outcomes over which an agent's preferences range in such a way that her preference over any two of these can be inferred from the utilities assigned to them. In particular, we assign utilities such that if outcome X involves greater utility than outcome Y, then the chooser prefers X to Y, and if outcome X and outcome Y involve the same utility, then the chooser is indifferent between X and Y.

Assuming an agent's preferences are coherent, and satisfy a few additional conditions, we can assign utilities to the outcomes over which her preferences range by plumbing her reflective evaluative attitudes.[2] Let her most-preferred outcome, X, be assigned a utility of 1, and her least-preferred outcome, Z, be assigned a utility of 0. Then the utility, u, of any other outcome over which her preferences range, Y, is equal to the value of p which would render her indifferent between Y and the lottery $[pX + (1-p)Z]$. By calculating the value of u for every Y, we can generate cardinal utilities for each outcome over which an agent's preferences range.

Referring to these cardinal utilities, we can arrange the possible outcomes of any of an agent's choices from most preferred to least preferred, obtaining a *preference ordering* over these outcomes. In transforming themselves, agents alter their preference orderings over the possible outcomes of the choice between acting justly and acting unjustly.

Transformation: Before and After

We shall assume that after implementing their conception of justice, contractors face an indeterminate number of pairwise interactions in which they must choose between acting justly and acting unjustly. Let C and D represent complying with and violating rules of justice during such an interaction respectively. Let pairs of letters represent the possible outcomes of any such interaction, with the letter on the left indicating the choice of the agent whose preferences we are considering, and the letter on the right indicating the choice of her partner. And let the ordering of these pairs from left to right represent an agent's ordering of the possible outcomes of any such pairwise interaction from most to least preferred.

Each of our contractors initially orders the possible outcomes of any pairwise interaction as follows: DC, CC, DD, CD.[3] These are PD preferences, so called because a pairwise interaction between agents who exhibit such preferences defines the standard prisoner's dilemma (PD).[4] In transforming herself, a contractor reranks these outcomes as follows: CC, CD, DC, DD. A contractor who has so transformed herself prefers outcomes in which she acts justly to all other possible outcomes of her interactions.

We can distinguish preferring something intrinsically, for itself, and preferring something instrumentally, for its power to cause something else. In transforming herself, a contractor comes to prefer intrinsically, and not instrumentally, outcomes in which she acts justly to outcomes in which she acts unjustly.

And we can distinguish an unconditional preference for acting justly rather than unjustly from one conditional on the expected compliance of others.[5] Self-transformation involves developing a preference of the former sort.

One might think that contractors with an unconditional preference to act justly rather than unjustly would be more vulnerable to exploitation than those with a conditional preference for doing so, and thus, that developing a preference of the former sort must be irrational. But there are several reasons to doubt that this is so.

First, even if contractors were to develop an unconditional preference for justice over injustice, their rules of justice might not require them to expose themselves to exploitation. In other words, these rules might themselves incorporate the sort of conditionality that would enable those following them to avoid being exploited.

Second, in some contexts, contractors might be able to avoid dangerous interactions entirely. The more fully they succeeded in doing so, the less vulnerable to exploitation an unconditional preference for justice over injustice would leave them relative to a conditional preference of this sort.

And third, as I shall argue, contractors would transform themselves only after empowering an enforcement mechanism offering them considerable protection against exploitation. Under such conditions, developing an unconditional preference to act justly rather than unjustly would expose contractors to only a limited risk of being exploited. And contractors are rational in accepting this limited risk, I shall argue, because they must transform themselves to maximize decision value. If this argument succeeds, then even under unconditional rules of justice requiring contractors to participate in dangerous interactions, developing an unconditional preference for acting justly rather than unjustly would be rational for contractors.

Let us say that agents who have developed the preference-ordering we have described exhibit *principled preferences*.

The Effects of Self-Transformation

Given their initial *PD* preferences, each of our contractors would do better treating her fellows unjustly than justly, no matter how she expects to be treated. Each is, accordingly, disposed to treat her fellows unjustly rather than justly. And being so disposed, each satisfies neither the compliance nor the motivation condition for possession of the sense of justice.

But having transformed herself, each would do better treating her fellows justly than unjustly, no matter how she expects to be treated. Each is, accordingly, disposed to treat her fellows justly rather than unjustly, satisfying the compliance condition. And preferring just to unjust actions intrinsically, each is disposed to treat her fellows justly rather than unjustly because she values doing so for its own sake, satisfying the motivation condition as well.

Alternative Representations of Self-Transformation

There are two other preference orderings the adoption of which would cause contractors to satisfy the compliance and motivation conditions: *CD, CC, DC, DD*, and *CC, CD, DD, DC*. So why characterize self-transformation as we have and not in terms of one of these other orderings?

Contractors would do better at satisfying their initial preferences by adopting *CC, CD, DC, DD* rather than *CD, CC, DC, DD*. Where contractors cannot affect their odds of ending up at *CC* rather than *CD*, those exhibiting either of these orderings can expect to do equally well by their initial preferences. But where contractors can affect their odds of ending up at *CC* rather than *CD*, those who have adopted *CC, CD, DC, DD* are most likely to realize the outcome they ranked second initially, while those who have adopted *CD, CC, DC, DD* are most likely to realize the outcome they ranked fourth initially.

And contractors would do better at satisfying their initial preferences were they to adopt *CC, CD, DC, DD* rather than *CC, CD, DD, DC*. Where contractors can act justly, those who exhibit either of these orderings can expect to do equally well by their initial preferences. But where contractors cannot act justly, those who have adopted *CC, CD, DC, DD* are most likely to realize the outcome they ranked first initially, while those who have adopted *CC, CD, DD, DC* are most likely to realize the outcome they ranked third initially.

Thus, we represent transformed contractors as having adopted *CC, CD, DC, DD* rather than either *CD, CC, DC, DD* or *CC, CD, DD, DC* because adopting either of the latter orderings over the former would be irrational for them.

Worries About the Justness of Transformed Contractors

Although transformed contractors satisfy the compliance and motivation conditions, one might nonetheless doubt that they exhibit the sense of justice, on the following grounds.

First, there is a long tradition associating justice with constraint.[6] In the spirit of this tradition, one might insist that for an action to count as just, it must involve some constraint on the part of the agent. Transformed contractors, however, do not constrain themselves at all in acting justly, for so acting assures them of realizing their first- or second-ranked outcome. Hence, they never act justly. And if they never act justly, transformed contractors do not exhibit the sense of justice.

Self-transformation, however, is consistent with the idea that justice involves constraint. Contractors have partially conflicting initial preferences. If all sought to maximize on these preferences, disputes among contractors would render each worse off than if all acted justly. Rules of justice, on this analysis, impose constraints on the initial preferences of contractors. Hence, acting justly, transformed contractors do constrain themselves. They constrain the pursuit of their initial preferences. Since self-transformation preserves a connection between justice and constraint, the above objection is mistaken.[7]

Second, one might worry that contractors who transform themselves for instrumental reasons value acting justly over acting unjustly for instrumental reasons as well, as a mere means to maximal satisfaction of their initial preferences. And appealing to the motivation condition, one might object that contractors who value acting justly over acting unjustly for instrumental reasons do not truly possess the sense of justice.

But this objection misunderstands the nature of self-transformation. Contractors transform themselves for instrumental reasons. But in transforming herself, a contractor initiates a causal process yielding an intrinsic preference for acting justly over acting unjustly. And having developed such a preference, she values acting justly rather than unjustly for its own sake, and not merely for instrumental reasons. That contractors fail to satisfy the motivation condition in becoming just does not imply that they would fail to do so after they have become just.

Third, one might think that an agent exhibits the sense of justice only if her disposition to act justly rather than unjustly is overriding. A transformed contractor has rearranged her preference ordering so that she prefers acting justly to acting unjustly. Such a transformation cannot, however, insure that nothing could ever induce such an agent to act unjustly. If, for instance, the probability that any of the actions available to a transformed contractor would put her in compliance with rules of justice were small enough, then violating these rules might promise her a higher utility than complying with them. And under such circumstances, such an agent would act unjustly. Pointing to this characteristic of transformed contractors, one might conclude that they lack the sense of justice.

It would, however, be a mistake to deny that transformed contractors exhibit the sense of justice on these grounds. For the rules of justice governing a community may bind its members only sometimes. And the times when temptation would induce transformed contractors to act in a (putatively) unjust manner may turn out to be times when their rules of justice fail to bind them. But even if transformed contractors would sometimes violate rules of justice when these rules bind them, this does not imply that they lack the sense of justice. For possession of the sense of justice, we do not require that an individual be completely impervious to temptation. Rather, we require that she be disposed to act justly rather than unjustly because she values doing so for its own sake, and that this disposition be efficacious under normal conditions.[8] And transformed contractors satisfy this requirement. Seeking to justify to members of our community what they regard as the sense of justice, there is no motivation for insisting that the sense of justice be overriding.

And finally, one might deny that transformed contractors exhibit the sense of justice because of worries about how enduring the effects of self-transformation are. Noting that contractors revise their initial preferences to advance them, one might worry that any time contractors could advance their initial preferences even further by revising their preferences again, they would do so. And appealing to this worry, one might claim that principled preferences are too transitory to constitute the sense of justice.

Transformed contractors are not, however, apt to revise their preferences any time they could maximize over their initial preferences by doing so. For transformed contractors retain their commitment to rationality. And on the conception of rationality we have assumed, this commitment would bring them to maximize over their present preferences, not their initial ones. Hence, the above objection is mistaken.

There are circumstances under which transformed contractors would revise their preferences.[9] Suppose, for instance, that by seeking to act justly, a transformed contractor diminished her odds of being in compliance with rules of justice. And suppose that for whatever reason, she expected this state of affairs to endure indefinitely. In this special (and perverse) case, a transformed contractor would maximize over her preferences by supplanting them. But since having the sense of justice is not rational *a priori*, cases such as this one do not warrant our refusing to attribute to transformed contractors the sense of justice.

Alternatives to Self-Transformation

Below, we differentiate self-transformation from previous attempts to establish that rational agents would act justly rather than unjustly for the right reasons, primarily by developing criticisms of these which self-transformation avoids.

Sen's Proposal

Amartya Sen concerns himself with trying to rationalize cooperation in the *PD*.[10] If we analyze the choice between acting justly and acting unjustly in terms of the *PD*, then Sen's proposal has implications for whether and why rational agents would be disposed to act justly rather than unjustly.

Sen identifies three sorts of preference orderings an agent engaged in a pairwise interaction might have. First, she might have *PD* preferences:

DC, CC, DD, CD.[11] Second, she might have Assurance Game (*AG*) preferences: *CC, DC, DD, CD*. Or third, she might have Other Regarding (*OR*) preferences: *CC, CD, DC, DD*.

Sen maintains that agents with *PD* preferences would not cooperate with one another, that those with *AG* preferences would do so under certain conditions, and that those with *OR* preferences would do so unconditionally. Having associated cooperation in the *PD* with acting morally, Sen ranks these three types of preferences from most to least moral: 1) *OR* preferences, 2) *AG* preferences, 3) *PD* preferences. He argues that by acting as if they had moral preferences, agents with *PD* preferences can satisfy their preferences more fully than they otherwise could. And on these grounds, Sen suggests that such agents should act as if they had *AG* or *OR* preferences. If Sen is right, then rational agents would be disposed to act justly rather than unjustly, at least given a *PD* analysis of the choice between these two options.

Self-transformation resembles Sen's proposal in several respects. Like Sen's proposal, it involves agents altering the basis on which they make their choices. Further, Sen argues for such alteration by appealing to its collective rationality, and I employ a similar strategy as part of an argument that our contractors would transform themselves. And finally, self-transformation involves acquiring what amount to *OR* preferences modified to range over the possible outcomes of pairwise interaction under rules of justice.

Sen's proposal, however, fails to establish that rational agents would be disposed to act justly rather than unjustly.[12] An agent with *PD* preferences always does better by defecting than by cooperating. Since an agent with *AG* or *OR* preferences would cooperate at least some of the time, rationality would preclude an agent with *PD* preferences from acting as if she had *AG* or *OR* preferences.[13]

But perhaps we should understand Sen's proposal differently. Perhaps agents are to supplement their *PD* preferences with, say, preferences to act as if they had *OR* preferences, then choose according to these "as if" preferences. Having done so, agents would appear to be disposed to cooperate with one another, for each has expanded her preference set to include a preference to act as if she preferred most of all so cooperating. Such "as if" preferences amount to preferences over outcomes, for they are not preferences to cooperate or defect unconditionally, but preferences to cooperate when another cooperates, cooperate when another defects, and so on. And so, an agent who has acquired a preference to choose as if she had *OR* preferences ranks outcomes as follows: *CC, CD, DC, DD*. Such an agent also retains her original *PD* ranking of outcomes: *DC, CC, DD, CD*. But an agent who ranks outcomes in both of these ways has ill-ordered preferences, preferring *DC* to *CC* while simultaneously preferring *CC* to *DC*, preferring *DC* to *CD* while simultaneously preferring *CD* to *DC*, and so on. And an agent who had supplemented her *PD* preferences with a preference to choose as if she had *AG* preferences would be similarly conflicted.

But perhaps we could avoid this impasse by requiring agents to supplement their *PD* preferences with higher-ranked preferences to choose as if they had *OR* preferences. Having done so, an agent exhibits the following preference ordering: 1) choose so as to contribute to the realization of *CC*, 2) choose . . . *CD*, 3) choose . . . *DC.*, 4) choose . . . *DD*, 5) *DC*, 6) *CC*, 7) *DD*, 8) *CD*. But a preference for a given outcome just is a preference to choose so as to contribute to the realization of this outcome. Thus, the above preference ordering is ill-ordered, for it ranks *CC* both first and sixth, *CD* both second and eighth, and so on. And an agent who had supplemented her *PD* preferences with a higher-ranked preference to choose as if she had *AG* preferences would be similarly conflicted.

Thus, no version of Sen's proposal yields agents with well-ordered preferences. And since agents with ill-ordered preferences cannot choose rationally, Sen's proposal cannot establish that rational agents would satisfy the compliance and motivation conditions on possession of the sense of justice.

Self-transformation avoids this difficulty. In transforming themselves, agents first transform their situation to render supplanting their *PD* preferences with principled preferences rational. Then they supplant their *PD* preferences with principled preferences. Having done so, they end up with a well-ordered set of preferences disposing them to act justly rather than unjustly because they value doing so for its own sake. Thus, unlike any version of Sen's proposal, self-transformation establishes that rational agents would satisfy both the compliance and motivation conditions.

Gauthier's Proposals

David Gauthier seeks to establish that rational agents would satisfy the compliance condition by appealing to constrained maximization, and that they would satisfy the motivation condition by appealing to an analysis of the sense of justice.[14]

Constrained Maximization. In the context of agreement on mutually beneficial rules of justice, *constrained maximization* is the disposition to comply with these rules when one expects others to do so, even if violating them promises one a greater payoff. Gauthier's argument for the rationality of this disposition is roughly the following. Assume translucency. Under such conditions, constrained maximizers can expect to enjoy more opportunities for cooperation than straightforward maximizers. As a result, they can expect to do better than straightforward maximizers at satisfying their preferences. Thus, it is rational for agents to acquire the disposition to maximize constrainedly. And since it is rational for agents to acquire this disposition, it is rational for them to act upon it, to act justly rather than unjustly when they expect others to do so.

Like constrained maximization, self-transformation assumes that rational agents can choose their dispositions, and that they would choose the ones promising them the highest payoff. But despite these similarities, self-transformation avoids several objections plaguing constrained maximization as an account of why rational agents would satisfy the compliance condition.

While Gauthier's agents are constructions, he generalizes his conclusions about them to actual individuals. Such a generalization is plausible only if these conclusions do not depend on Gauthier's attributing to his contractors some feature we cannot reasonably attribute to actual agents.

But some have claimed that the degree of translucency Gauthier attributes to his contractors is just such a feature:

> it is fantastic to suppose that while walking down the street a real person who is a CM [constrained maximizer] (assuming that there really are CMs) can reliably spot his fellows twice as often as he fails.[15]

Others have worried that among actual individuals, maintaining the degree of translucency assumed by Gauthier's argument for constrained maximization would involve costs not reflected in this argument. Peter Danielson has argued that maintaining such a degree of translucency would involve differential costs for constrained and straightforward maximizers, and predicted that taking this into account, we would find that cooperation among the two would yield a mixed equilibrium.[16] And Robert Frank has constructed simple models establishing that unless dispositions are readable without cost to the readers, cooperation between constrained and straightforward maximizers would yield just such an equilibrium.[17] In the face of these results, Gauthier's argument retains its force only among agents who exhibit what we cannot reasonably attribute to actual individuals, the ability to read one another's dispositions costlessly.

Taken together, the above concerns suggest the following objection to Gauthier's argument for constrained maximization: while it may show that contractors translucent in just Gauthier's sense should satisfy the compliance condition, we cannot plausibly generalize this conclusion to actual individuals. Thus, an appeal to constrained maximization fails to establish that actual individuals, even rational ones, should be disposed to act justly rather than unjustly.

Self-transformation is not vulnerable to a similar charge. Transformed agents prefer outcomes in which they act justly to all other possible outcomes of their interactions. And for such agents, information about the dispositions of others is simply irrelevant to the choice between acting justly and acting unjustly. Hence, an appeal to self-transformation, unlike an appeal to constrained maximization, can show that actual individuals should be disposed to choose just over unjust actions no matter how translucent they are, and no matter how much maintaining translucency costs.

The most serious objections to constrained maximization challenge its rationality. Gauthier claims that constrained maximization requires agents to perform only rational actions. Many, however, have argued that constrained maximization is no more than a rationally adopted disposition to perform irrational actions.[18] Duncan MacIntosh's argument is fairly typical.[19]

Assume, with Gauthier, that an action is rational just in case required by a disposition it maximizes to adopt. Now initially, it maximizes to adopt a disposition to maximize constrainedly, for when others see it, they will cooperate with its possessor. But after an agent has adopted this disposition, when it comes time to act, it no longer maximizes to possess it, for she could do even better if she possessed a disposition to maximize straightforwardly. But then such an agent should dispose herself to maximize straightforwardly, which renders actions required by constrained maximization irrational by Gauthier's own standard.

Nor would it help to stipulate that constrained maximization involves adopting an irrevocable disposition which would force its possessor to maximize constrainedly. For in acting from such a disposition, even one which was rationally adopted, an agent does not act freely and rationally. Rather, she is caused to act irrationally by a disposition it was once rational to adopt, but which is no longer the rational one to have and to act upon. Again, constrained maximization turns out to be irrational action required by a rationally adopted disposition. And as such, it cannot explain why rational agents would satisfy the compliance condition.

The same cannot be said of self-transformation. For transformed agents have come to prefer outcomes in which they act justly to all other possible outcomes of their actions. And having so revised her preferences, an agent acts so as to realize her most preferred outcome by acting justly rather than unjustly. Hence, self-transformation, unlike constrained maximization, requires agents to perform only maximizing actions.

Gauthier proposes constrained maximization as a means of closing the gap between rationality and compliance with moral rules, but it has implications for motivation as well. For a constrained maximizer, that some action is required by a rational disposition provides her with sufficient reason to perform it. And it is rational to have a disposition to act justly rather than unjustly, or so we shall argue. Thus, that an action is just provides a constrained maximizer with sufficient reason to perform it. And thus, constrained maximizers are disposed to act justly rather than unjustly because doing so is just.[20]

Constrained maximizers are not, however, disposed to act justly rather than unjustly because they value doing so for its own sake. What makes them constrained maximizers, after all, is that they prefer acting unjustly to acting justly. Thus, unlike transformed agents, they do not satisfy the motivation condition for possession of the sense of justice.

One might think that this difference is trivial. But among agents flawed as we are, it is not. Wishful thinking might cause an agent who does not value acting justly rather than unjustly for its own sake to see an unjust action as a just action, and to act accordingly. Or selective perception might bring such an agent to overlook facts she requires to determine correctly what justice requires of her, and to act accordingly. But such distortions could not bring an agent who values acting justly over acting unjustly for its own sake to act justly rather than unjustly. For such an agent, there is no gap between doing what she wishes and acting justly rather than unjustly, or between seeing what she wishes and perceiving what justice requires of her. Thus, as the result of their differing motivations, constrained maximizers are disposed to act justly less frequently, and unjustly more frequently, than transformed agents.

The Sense of Justice.   But perhaps we should not treat constrained maximization as an attempt to show that rational agents would be disposed to do the right thing for the right reason. After all, Gauthier developed constrained maximization as an account of the rationality of moral compliance. Recently, he has addressed the issue of motivation directly by developing an account of the sense of justice. Perhaps an appeal to this account can establish that rational agents would satisfy the motivation condition.

Gauthier proposes that we think of individuals as naturally possessing the sense of justice, a disposition which 1) motivates compliance with terms of social cooperation, and 2) involves valuing participation in just social arrangements intrinsically. On Gauthier's analysis, the sense of justice develops from a prereflective disposition towards conformity, but it is rationalized by prudence. It is valuable to its possessors because it makes them attractive to others as partners in mutually beneficial cooperation.

Both Gauthier and I conceive of the sense of justice as a disposition to act justly rather than unjustly because one values doing so intrinsically. There is, nonetheless, an important difference in our treatments of the sense of justice.

On Gauthier's account, the sense of justice is not derived from, based in, or constituted by an agent's preferences. Rather, it is a disposition distinct from an agent's preferences, an independent source of reasons for action. So understood, the sense of justice provides an agent with a noninstrumental reason for action, one entering her deliberation directly, unmediated by her preferences. As Gauthier puts it, the sense of justice provides its possessor with a reason for action which is "simply and straightforwardly a reason to be just."[21]

But this move to motivational pluralism insures that within the circumstances of justice, Gauthier's just agents are conflicted. The sense of justice provides them with reasons to act justly, while their preferences provide them with reasons to act unjustly. This conflict threatens to reopen the compliance problem among possessors of the sense of justice. For agents who perceive themselves as having reasons to act unjustly remain prepared to act unjustly whenever their reasons for acting justly lapse. But worse than this, they cannot resolve this conflict by appealing to instrumental rationality. For instrumental rationality has nothing to say about choosing among reasons for action when these are not themselves ordered according to the potential consequences of acting on them for preference satisfaction. Thus, if agents let the reasons provided by Gauthier's sense of justice guide their actions, their choice to do so is not a rational one, and an appeal to it cannot establish that rational agents would satisfy the motivation condition.

In the spirit of Gauthier's earlier work, one might argue that the sense of justice is a rational disposition because possessing it, an agent can expect to maximize. Conjoined to the claim that an action is rational if required by a rational disposition, this would imply that acting from Gauthier's sense of justice is rational.

But this argument is flawed in the same manner as Gauthier's defense of the rationality of constrained maximization. When an agent's preferences and Gauthier's sense of justice diverge in their recommendations, as they do each time she interacts within the circumstances of justice, possessing this disposition no longer maximizes for her. Under these conditions, Gauthier's sense of justice is no longer a rational disposition, and it is not longer rational, even by Gauthier's standards, to do what it requires.

On self-transformation, contrastingly, the sense of justice is a well-ordered set of preferences with a particular content. As such, it provides transformed agents with reasons for action of a kind with those provided by their other preferences. And such agents can sort out any conflicts among their reasons for action by appealing to instrumental rationality. Thus, unlike possessors of Gauthier's sense of justice, transformed agents are not conflicted, and an appeal to their choices can establish that rational agents would satisfy the motivation condition.

McClennen's Proposal

E. F. McClennen maintains that in at least some situations, agents ought to discipline their present choices to plans adopted in the past. This account of resolute choice is part of a more general theory of dynamic rational choice.[22] We shall sketch this theory, locate resolute choice and self-transformation within it, and then consider the relative merits of each as accounts of why rational agents would satisfy the compliance and motivation conditions. We begin by introducing some terminology required to describe McClennen's theory of dynamic rational choice.

A *dynamic decision problem* is a sequence of choice points, with the options available at each point in this sequence depending on the choice made at the previous point, or on some chance event, or on some combination of the two. A *plan* specifies a sequence of such options that can be implemented. Thus for each choice point in such a sequence, a plan specifies a choice from among those options available given 1) what was chosen at the preceding choice point, and 2) each possible combination of chance events, if any, since the preceding choice point. A *prospect* is the expected outcome associated with a plan.

For every dynamic decision problem, there is a set of possible plans, any one of which may be actualized by the agent's choices. Further, for every such problem, there is a set of possible terminal outcomes, one of which will be actualized by the agent's choices and any chance events which occur. Prospects relate possible plans to possible terminal outcomes.

For any set of such prospects, we shall assume that there is a subset of prospects defined over outcomes an agent evaluates as acceptable. An acceptable set of prospects can guide choice only if an agent can use it to pick out an acceptable plan. But how are we to determine what plans are acceptable? McClennen proposes four conditions on acceptable plans.

The first of these is *Simple Reduction (SR)*. It states that if each of the plans available in a dynamic decision problem may be implemented by a single initial choice, then for each plan s and its associated prospect g, s is in the acceptable set of plans if and only if g is in the acceptable set of prospects. That is, the acceptability of a simple, one-shot plan should depend on the acceptability of its associated prospect.

SR explicates a presupposition of all instrumental accounts of rationality, that agents ought to base their choices on an evaluation of the prospects of these choices. For this reason, we shall not question McClennen's claim that *SR* is the least controversial of the conditions on dynamic rational choice, taking it as a given that acceptable plans must satisfy it.[23]

In a typical dynamic decision problem, plans can be implemented only through a sequence of choices, so that *SR* alone does not suffice to guide choice. For every such plan, we can define its *normal form* version as the one in which all of its components are implemented by a single initial choice. The contrast here is with the *extensive form* version of that same plan, the version in which each of its components are implemented sequentially. With this background, we can introduce McClennen's second condition on acceptable plans. *Normal Form/Extensive Form Coincidence (NEC)* states that in any dynamic decision problem, any plan *s* belongs to the acceptable set of plans if and only if its normal form version *s'* belongs to the acceptable set of normal form plans. That is, it should make no difference if we offer an agent a choice among terminal outcomes as a one-time choice or as a sequence of choices.

At each point in a sequence of choices, an agent may consider the set of truncated plans available to her at that point, where a *truncated plan* is a sequence of choices beginning from that choice point. An agent may also consider the set of plan continuations available to her at each point in a sequence of choices, with a *plan continuation* being the continuation of a plan initially available to her. Given these distinctions, we can formulate McClennen's third condition on acceptable plans. For any plan *s* and any choice point *n* that can be reached by following *s*, let *s(n)* be the truncated plan specifying the same choices as the continuation of *s* at *n*. According to *Dynamic Consistency (DC)*, for any choice point *n* and any plan *s* in a dynamic decision problem, if *n* can be reached by following *s*, then *s(n)* belongs to the set of truncated plans acceptable at *n* if and only if *s* belongs to the set of initially acceptable plans. Intuitively, *DC* requires that an agent not change her mind about the acceptability of a plan during its execution.

At each point in a sequence of choices, an agent may also consider what would be acceptable to her if that point defined the beginning of a choice problem. For any choice point *n*, this is the *de novo* choice problem at *n*. For every truncated plan *s(n)* available at *n* in a choice problem, there is a plan *s*n* available in the *de novo* choice problem at *n*. *Separability (SEP)* states that for any choice point *n* and any truncated plan *s(n)*, *s(n)* is in the set of acceptable truncated plans at *n* if and only if the corresponding plan *s*n* is in the set of acceptable *de novo* plans at *n*. In plain terms, *SEP* requires that an agent choose at each choice point in a dynamic decision problem as if she were starting over, selecting a plan *de novo*.

In any given dynamic decision problem, an agent committed to *SR* may evaluate terminal outcomes in such a way that she violates none of *DC*, *NEC*, and *SEP*. But there are dynamic choice problems in which agents committed to *SR* who evaluate terminal outcomes in certain ways must violate at least one of these conditions. Here is one such problem.[24]

Ulysses is ready to return to Ithaca.[25] To get there, he must pass the Sirens. Unlike the Sirens of the original myth, these do not exert an irresistible compulsion on hearers. Rather, their song alters the preferences of hearers so that they choose, in the normal manner, to sail to their doom. Before embarking, Ulysses prefers to sail straight to Ithaca, and to avoid the Isle of the Sirens. Upon hearing the Sirens, however, his preferences will change so that he prefers changing course for the Isle of the Sirens to sailing on to Ithaca. Ulysses is aware of all of these things.

There are only three plans available to Ulysses for sailing to Ithaca consistent with *SR*. First, he might sail for Ithaca, then change course for the Isle of the Sirens upon hearing their song. This plan violates *DC*, which requires that an agent not change her mind about the acceptability of a plan during its execution. Second, Ulysses might sail for Ithaca, but have his sailors bind him to the mast and stop up their ears, so that he cannot respond to the Sirens' song. This plan violates *NEC*. For were Ulysses to choose among normal-form versions of his available plans, he would reject the normal-form version of this plan in favor of sailing unbound to Ithaca despite hearing the Sirens' song. And third, Ulysses might sail unbound to Ithaca despite hearing the Sirens' song. To do so, however, is to choose differently upon hearing this song than he would *de novo*, that is, to violate *SEP*. Hence, whichever of the above plans that Ulysses implements, he must violate one of *DC*, *NEC*, and *SEP*.

Unless we dismiss Ulysses as irrational, a charge instrumentalism will not support, we must admit that in some situations, a rational agent committed to *SR* cannot choose in accordance with all of *DC*, *NEC*, and *SEP*. To guide choice within such situations, a conception of dynamic rationality must relax at least one of these three conditions on acceptable plans.

Resolute choice involves a commitment to *SR*, *DC*, and *NEC*, and a rejection of *SEP*. To choose resolutely, an agent resolves to follow the plan which seems best to her initially within a dynamic decision problem. And having so resolved, she follows this plan even when departing from it would yield her prospects more attractive, considered *de novo*, than those associated with the plan she has resolved to follow. In this manner, by virtue of their commitment to *NEC* over *SEP*, resolute choosers discipline their present choices to their past choices.

Sophisticated choice, of which self-transformation is a form, involves a commitment to *SR*, *DC*, and *SEP*, and a rejection of *NEC*. To choose sophisticatedly, an agent looks ahead to what option will seem best to her considered *de novo* at each choice point, then rejects any plans requiring her to choose something she would disprefer *de novo*. In this manner, by virtue of their commitment to *SEP* over *NEC*, sophisticated choosers discipline their future choices to their present choices.

Having resolved to choose just over unjust actions, a resolute chooser prefers acting justly to acting unjustly intrinsically, even though she prefers acting unjustly to acting justly intrinsically *de novo*. And a rational agent with such preferences chooses just over unjust actions because she values doing so for its own sake. Thus, resolute choice, like self-transformation, can account for rational agents satisfying the compliance and motivation conditions.

Transformed agents and resolute choosers share a commitment to *SR* and *DC*. But because transformed agents reject *NEC* in favor of *SEP*, while resolute choosers reject *SEP* in favor of *NEC*, the two accounts are not subject to precisely the same worries. To differentiate them, we shall develop two worries about resolute choice as an account of why rational agents would satisfy the compliance and motivation conditions.

First, by appealing to the possibility that an agent would not remain the same person throughout a decision problem, one might argue that there are conditions under which choosing resolutely is irrational.

There are three plausible accounts of when *A* and *B* are the same person: 1) when *A* and *B* have the same immaterial soul, 2) when *A* is uniquely psychologically related to *B*, 3) when enough of *A*'s brain has continued to exist as *B*'s brain for *B* to survive as a person, and this continuity is non-branching.[26]

On the first account, an agent ceases to persist as the same person if her soul is exchanged for some other soul. On the second, an agent who has suffered a serious enough head injury, stroke, or neurological disorder does not remain the same person. And on the third, if the psychological relations comprising identity become sufficiently attenuated, an agent is not who she was. Thus, on all three of these accounts, an agent might become a different person at some point during a decision problem.

Further, since all three of these accounts exhibit significant failings, agents cannot be certain which is correct.[27] Thus, in any decision problem where the three accounts disagree about the relationship between the agent entering a decision problem and the agent moving through it, there is uncertainty as to whether these two agents are one and the same person.

Within any given decision problem, *NEC* requires an agent to discipline each of her choices to the plan she judged most acceptable initially. In some decision problems, whether the agent executing a plan is the same person as the agent initiating this plan is uncertain. In others, it is certain, on any plausible account of personal identity, that the agent executing a plan is not the same person as the agent initiating it. And if an agent has become a different person at some point during a decision problem, then to reject *SEP* in favor of *NEC* is to let the preferences of someone other than herself guide her choices.

Instrumental rationality requires, at a minimum, that the preferences guiding an agent's choices be her own. Thus, if there is sufficient uncertainty as to whether an agent has persisted as the same person throughout a decision problem, or if it is certain that she has not, choosing resolutely is not rational for her. And thus, an appeal to resolute choice fails to establish that rational agents would satisfy the compliance and motivation conditions over the whole range of conditions under which they might choose.

Self-transformation is not subject to the same worry. Because transformed agents always choose as if they were choosing *de novo*, their present preferences always ratify their choices. Every agent can be assured that her present preferences are her own, for at any given time, an agent is (trivially) the same person as herself at that time. Thus, by rejecting *NEC* in favor of *SEP*, transformed agents insure that the preferences guiding their choices are their own.

And second, resolute choice fails to establish that all ideally rational agents would satisfy the compliance and motivation conditions.

McClennen offers a pragmatic argument for choosing resolutely.[28] In some contexts, resolute choosers do better than *myopic choosers*, characterized by a commitment to *SR*, *NEC*, and *SEP* over *DC*, because myopic choosers cannot execute any plans requiring them to choose initially dispreferred actions.[29] And in some contexts, resolute choosers do better than sophisticated choosers, because the former, unlike the latter, can realize their most-preferred outcomes without paying any precommitment costs.[30] But there are no contexts in which resolute choosers would do worse than either myopic choosers or sophisticated choosers. For suppose that some plan under consideration by a resolute chooser were dominated by some other plan, one which would be executed by a myopic or sophisticated chooser. Under such circumstances, a resolute chooser would always adopt the dominant plan, for a resolute chooser just is an agent who adopts the plan she judges best initially, then disciplines her subsequent choices to this plan. Thus, resolute choosers do at least as well as other choosers in all contexts, and better than other choosers in some contexts.

Appealing to this pragmatic argument, McClennen explains how resolute choosers come to prefer to do what they have resolved to do. A preference change is *endogenous* if an agent's commitment to rationality alone causes it. On McClennen's view, the recognition of the pragmatic argument for choosing resolutely rather than in some other manner causes a resolute chooser's preferences to change endogenously in accordance with the requirements of NEC. So viewed, res-

olute choice involves a frictionless, and thus costless, shuffling of conative attitudes.

If we grant the truth of McClennen's pragmatic argument, an appeal to
endogenous preference change establishes that deeply rational agents
can choose resolutely.[31] But if an agent's preferences do not respond
spontaneously, automatically, and directly to rational criticism, recognition of a pragmatic argument for choosing resolutely will not bring her
preferences into line with the requirements of *NEC*. Thus, an appeal to
endogenous preference change fails to establish that shallowly rational
agents can choose resolutely. And thus, an appeal to resolute choice fails
to establish that our shallowly rational contractors would satisfy the compliance and motivation conditions. Because self-transformation does not
assume direct, spontaneous, and automatic preference revision, it is not
subject to the same worry.

A defender of resolute choice might reply to these objections in kind,
arguing that self-transformation is subject to a number of worries to
which resolute choice is not.

One might argue that the ability to commit to plans benefits agents,
and that a commitment to *SEP* over *NEC* makes it impossible for agents
to commit to plans.[32] But surely this is not so, for several accounts of plan-
following consistent with a commitment to *SEP* over *NEC* have been developed. On Ainslie's account, agents who take present violation of a
plan as setting a precedent for future violations of similar plans can commit themselves to plans for forward-looking reasons.[33] And Bratman appeals to a rational presumption against reconsidering prior plans to argue
that agents committed to *SEP* over *NEC* can commit themselves to
plans.[34] An appeal to such accounts establishes that a commitment to *SEP*
over *NEC*, like the one exhibited by transformed agents, does not preclude agents from committing to plans.

Alternatively, one might object to sophisticated choice by appealing to
cases in which an agent must pick between equally acceptable options.[35]
Suppose that facing two such options, an agent decides to flip a coin. She
correlates one outcome with "heads" and the other with "tails," flips the
coin, and it comes up "heads. If she is committed to *SEP* over *NEC*, this
event provides her with no reason to choose one option over the other, for
SEP requires her to ignore everything but future consequences in choosing, including the lie of a coin tossed in the past. Thus, it appears that
agents committed to *SEP* over *NEC* cannot break ties of indifference.
They end up like Buridan's ass, unable to choose between options any
one of which would be an improvement on their situation. By appealing
to the plausible claim that such cases are ubiquitous among us, one might
argue that we should reject sophisticated choice in favor of resolute
choice on instrumental grounds.

We answer this objection by accepting the distinction between choosing and picking while restricting the scope of *SEP*. The two activities, after all, are distinct. Choosing involves selecting among options valued differentially, while picking involves selecting among options valued equally. We claim that there are distinct norms governing these distinct activities. *SEP* governs rational choosing, but not rational picking.

But perhaps this defense of sophisticated choice is *ad hoc*. One might think that the conditions on selecting rationally among alternatives should be the same across different types of evaluative orderings. After all, what could justify requiring agents to satisfy *SEP* when choosing among strictly preferred options, but not options regarded with indifference?[36]

If an agent is picking among equally acceptable options, there are no differences in the value of these options to which she could possibly respond. There is, thus, no instrumental rationale for accepting *SEP* as a condition on picking. Indeed, if the above complaint about *SEP* is right, there is an instrumental rationale for rejecting *SEP* as a condition on picking. Thus, far from being *ad hoc*, our refusal to extend *SEP* from choosing to picking is required by our commitment to instrumental rationality. And thus, *SEP*'s failure as a condition on rational picking does not imply that we should reject sophisticated choice in favor of resolute choice on instrumental grounds.

MacIntosh's Proposal

Duncan MacIntosh tries to rehabilitate Gauthier's account of constrained maximization by developing a proposal about preference revision.[37]

He suggests that in the *PD*, rational agents should acquire the preferences it would maximize for them to have, given their initial preferences, and then choose actions from these new preferences.[38] And MacIntosh maintains that rational agents would maximize in the *PD* if they preferred for its own sake cooperating with others who are similarly disposed. Accordingly, he recommends that parties to the *PD* replace their initial preferences with the following preferences: 1) defect against (i) anyone who has, will, or likely will defect, (ii) unconditional cooperators, and (iii) unconditional defectors; 2) have outcome *CC*; 3) cooperate with just (iv) those disposed to choose as if their first two preferences were 1) and 2) and who do not fit (i); 4) have outcome *DC* with those who satisfy (iv); 5) have outcome *CD*.[39]

Extending this recommendation to the circumstances of justice, we can account for rational agents satisfying the compliance and motivation conditions. Having adopted rules of justice, they should rank first acting justly except when faced with those who have acted unjustly in the past, those who prefer unconditionally to act unjustly, or those who prefer unconditionally to act justly. If all rational members of a community acquired this ranking, and all knew one another to have acquired it, all would be disposed to choose just over unjust actions, satisfying the compliance condition trivially. And all would act justly rather than unjustly under these conditions, because all would rank doing so over their other options.

Both MacIntosh's proposal and self-transformation require agents with *PD* preferences to reorder their preferences so that they rank acting justly over acting unjustly, at least under some conditions. And both explain why rational parties to the *PD* involved in acting justly rather than unjustly would satisfy the compliance and motivation conditions by appealing to straightforward maximization over revised preferences. Nonetheless, the two proposals differ significantly. To establish this, we shall develop several worries about MacIntosh's proposal as an account of why rational agents would satisfy the compliance and motivation conditions.

First, one might object that MacIntosh's revised preferences would not dispose agents to choose justice over injustice in a wide enough array of circumstances to count as the sense of justice. For MacIntosh's revised preferences commit an agent to acting unjustly whenever she interacts with someone known to prefer unconditionally to act justly. And even if one grants that defensive violations are consistent with possession of the sense of justice, one might deny that agents who violate rules of justice offensively exhibit this disposition. Since transformed contractors develop a preference for choosing justice over injustice whatever their perceptions of the dispositions of others, self-transformation is not vulnerable to a similar objection.

Second, the revised preferences MacIntosh recommends are, for the most part, preferences to treat agents with certain dispositions justly, and to treat other agents unjustly. But an agent can only differentiate the dispositions of sufficiently translucent agents. As we have seen, the degree to which actual individuals are translucent, and how much it would cost them to maintain the degree of translucency required by MacIntosh's argument, are controversial issues. And in the face of such controversy, one might worry about the plausibility of generalizing MacIntosh's results to actual agents, even rational ones. Because self-transformation need not presuppose that agents exhibit any particular degree of translucency, it is not subject to a similar worry.

And third, MacIntosh's proposal assumes an account of preference revision which is not feasible for all ideally rational agents. According to MacIntosh, preference revision among such agents is direct, spontaneous, and automatic.[40] For an ideally rational agent's preferences to change, she need only realize that such a change would cause the conditions targeted in her original preferences. This is, of course, exactly how preference revision works among deeply rational agents. But shallowly rational agents have perceptual, mnemonic, cognitive, and psychological limitations which preclude direct, spontaneous, and automatic revision of their intrinsic preferences. Thus, an appeal to MacIntosh's proposal cannot establish that our shallowly rational contractors would be disposed to choose justice over injustice because they value doing so for its own sake. But self-transformation is not subject to the same worry. Because it does not assume direct, spontaneous, and automatic preference revision, self-transformation can establish that shallowly rational agents, as well as deeply rational ones, would satisfy the compliance and motivation conditions on possession of the sense of justice.

Danielson's Proposal

Peter Danielson proposes to establish that rational agents would be disposed to act morally rather than immorally by appealing to his account of artificial morality.[41] To do so, Danielson constructs various types of artificial agents, then pits them against one another pairwise in a series of single-play *PD*s. One such agent is the reciprocal cooperator, who cooperates if and only if doing so is both necessary and sufficient to induce a cooperative response in others. Danielson argues that under conditions of costless transparency, reciprocal cooperators would do better at advancing their interests than agents of any other type, so that instrumentally rational agents would become reciprocal cooperators.[42] Arguing that reciprocal cooperation is a moral principle, albeit a minimal one, Danielson concludes that instrumentally rational agents would be disposed to treat one another morally rather than immorally. And they would be so disposed because they have adopted a recognizably moral principle.

There are some important similarities between artificial morality and self-transformation. First, both model the choice between whether or not to act justly as a series of single-play *PD*s played by rational agents. Second, both operate with a "dirty" conception of rational agents. Danielson's agents lack knowledge of one another's preferences, and they are not equally rational. Our contractors also lack knowledge of one another's preferences. And although they are equally rational, they suffer differentially from perceptual, mnemonic, cognitive, and psychological flaws. And third, both artificial morality and self-transformation involve agents transforming themselves so as to advance their ends as much as they possibly can. Our contractors transform their preferences, Danielson's agents the principles which determine their actions.[43] Nonetheless, the two proposals differ significantly. To establish this, we shall develop several worries about artificial morality as an account of why rational agents would satisfy the compliance and motivation conditions on possession of the sense of justice.

First, unlike our contractors, Danielson's agents are not constructed so as to capture our own psychological features. They are transparent to the point of being able to read one another's minds, given permission. There are no bounds on their computational or mnemonic abilities. They make no mistakes. And each can be given the power to rewrite the principles that govern its behavior without delay or cost. An argument that such agents should dispose themselves to act justly rather than unjustly for the right reason cannot be plausibly generalized to members of our community, even rational ones.[44] And we can so generalize an argument that our contractors should become just, or so we shall argue.

Second, artificial morality fails to establish that agents would be disposed to treat all of their fellows justly rather than unjustly.[45] The substantive conclusion of artificial morality is that rational parties to the *PD* would become reciprocal cooperators. And reciprocal cooperators defect on anyone they identify as an unconditional cooperator. But even if one grants that defensive violations are consistent with possession of the sense of justice, one might deny that agents who violate rules of justice offensively exhibit this disposition. Since transformed contractors develop a preference for acting justly rather than unjustly whatever their perceptions of the dispositions of others, self-transformation is not vulnerable to a similar objection.

And third, Danielson's agents would not satisfy the motivation condition to the same extent as transformed agents. Danielson argues that reciprocal cooperation is a moral principle. And he defines morality as requiring constraint on preference satisfaction. Thus, at least some of the time, reciprocal cooperators choose right over wrong against the balance of their preferences, contravening the motivation condition. Contrastingly, transformed agents satisfy the motivation condition whenever they choose justice over injustice, because they value doing so intrinsically.

Thus, an appeal to artificial morality establishes a weaker link between rationality and moral motivation than an appeal to self-transformation. And among agents like us, the strength of this link matters. For as we have seen, flawed agents who value acting justly rather than unjustly for its own sake would violate rules of justice less frequently than flawed agents who do not.

Objections to Preference Revision

Having differentiated self-transformation from previous attempts to establish that rational agents would satisfy the compliance and motivation conditions on possession of the sense of justice, we shall consider a number of objections to the very idea of self-transformation. Only if we can answer these objections can we call upon self-transformation in justifying the sense of justice to individuals.

First, one might object that self-transformation amounts to stoicism.[46] This is the view that one should not care about what happens, or should not care that things do not happen as one wants them to happen, or should care only that things will happen as they will inevitably happen. Were self-transformation equivalent to stoicism, rational members of our community would be right to reject it, for it would render them less effective at pursuing their initial preferences.

Both stoicism and self-transformation involve agents seeking to increase the congruence between their preferences and the world by changing their preferences. But the resemblance between the two ends here. On stoicism, agents give up satisfying their initial preferences, coming to prefer that the world be as it is. On self-transformation, agents acquire preferences the possession of which will advance their prior preferences. By changing their preferences, they bring the world closer to how they prefer it to be. Hence, unlike stoicism, self-transformation never requires agents to abdicate the pursuit of what they presently prefer.

Second, one might object that self-transformation undermines the possibility of rational choice.[47] For rational choice involves seeking to satisfy a particular set of preferences as fully as one can. Self-transformation, however, asserts that agents ought to change certain of their preferences, implying that their preferences are not fixed. But if their preferences are not fixed, then how can rational agents maximize over them?

Rational choice requires only that agents have a set of preferences which is fixed at each moment of choice, not a set which does not change over time. And since agents have a determinate set of preferences before, during, and after self-transformation, it satisfies this prerequisite for rational choice. Thus, self-transformation does not undermine the conditions necessary for rational choice.

Third, one might worry that seeking to satisfy preferences by changing them can never be rational.[48] After all, having transformed herself, an agent no longer possesses the preferences she transformed herself in order to satisfy maximally. And she cannot derive any satisfaction from maximizing over a set of preferences if she no longer possesses it. One might think that rationality prohibits agents from choosing so as to undercut the possibility of their own future satisfaction, and so prohibits self-transformation.

As we have described self-transformation, however, it does not involve agents replacing their preferences wholesale. In transforming herself, an agent retains all of the interests defined by her initial preferences, she just comes to regard the pursuit of these interests as less important than acting justly rather than unjustly. And having so reordered her preferences, an agent would still derive satisfaction from maximizing over her initial preferences.

More importantly, however, this objection misunderstands the nature of preference satisfaction on instrumentalism. Let us distinguish between satisfaction, the obtaining of that for which one has a preference, and the feeling of satisfaction an agent gets when her present preferences are satisfied. Instrumentalism requires agents to maximize the expected satisfaction of their present preferences, not to maximize the amount of satisfaction they feel.[49] Since we are operating with a version of instrumentalism, it is no objection to self-transformation that it requires agents to choose in a way expected to yield a smaller amount of satisfaction than they might otherwise feel.

Fourth, one might object that self-transformation requires agents to revise their preferences on demand, but that agents cannot control the content of their preferences. Preferences are something with which agents are just born, or develop in the course of their lives through nonrational processes. Appealing to this conception of preferences, one might object to self-transformation on the grounds that it incorrectly treats preferences as being within the voluntary control of agents.

But even if preferences change only through nonrational processes, agents can yet choose whether or not to initiate such processes. And self-transformation, as we shall describe it, involves preference change through nonrational processes which can be initiated voluntarily by rational agents. Thus, self-transformation treats as voluntary only those aspects of preference change which can be plausibly treated as voluntary.

Fifth, one might object that self-transformation conflates instrumental and intrinsic value. On self-transformation, agents develop the sense of justice for instrumental reasons. Further, instrumental considerations rationalize their maintaining this disposition. But one might worry that an agent who develops the sense of justice for instrumental reasons, and whose grounds for maintaining this disposition are instrumental, cannot be said to value acting justly rather than unjustly intrinsically. Indeed, one might think that we can attribute the sense of justice to such an agent only by mistaking her instrumentally-grounded concern to act justly rather than unjustly for a concern to do so for its own sake.

The confusion here is in the objection.[50] There is a difference between preferring something for instrumental reasons and having instrumental reasons for developing and maintaining a preference for something. One can have instrumental reasons for developing and maintaining a preference which is not itself instrumental. On self-transformation, agents have instrumental reasons for initiating a causal process which results in their valuing just action more than unjust action intrinsically. And having completed this process, they have instrumental reasons, deriving from their revised preferences, for not reversing it. Thus, transformed agents develop and maintain for instrumental reasons a preference which is not itself instrumental. And thus, self-transformation involves no conflation of instrumental and intrinsic value.

And finally, one might object to self-transformation because of worries about personal identity.[51] If two persons have different preferences, then they are not identical to one another. Appealing to this truism, one might argue that in transforming herself, an agent becomes a new and different person, one who is not identical to the person she was. And one might think that since self-transformation entails the end of the agent transforming herself, it could not be rational for anyone, or at least not for anyone the satisfaction of whose present preferences requires her continued existence.

This objection presupposes that an agent at one time is the same person as an agent at another time only if the two have precisely the same properties. But this is impossible, since all such agents differ in at least one property, their temporal locations. Hence, if we think that persons can persist over time, we must reject the above account of personal identity.

But there are more plausible accounts of when A and B are the same person. Indeed, we have identified three: 1) when A and B have the same immaterial soul, 2) when A is uniquely psychologically related to B, 3) when enough of A's brain has continued to exist as B's brain for B to survive as a person, and this continuity is non-branching. To sustain the above objection, one would have to show that self-transformation entails a loss of identity on one of these three accounts.

Since an agent can revise her preferences without necessarily altering her soul, self-transformation does not entail a loss of identity on the first account.

Since an agent can revise her preferences without altering her brain so much that she cannot survive as a person, self-transformation does not entail a loss of identity on the second account.

Determining whether an agent can survive preference revision on the third account requires more analysis. Let us say that A is psychologically related to B just in case 1) the psychological states of A are continuous with those of B, and 2) this continuity is caused in the right way.[52] Continuity consists in the holding of overlapping chains of enough direct psychological connections. Caused in the right way, it develops as the result of normal psychological processes, not through brainwashing, neurological tampering, unsolicited hypnosis, or the like.

Self-transformation does not entail a violation of the first of these requirements. Having preferences which persist from one moment to the next is only one sort of direct psychological connection. Other sorts, direct and indirect memory connections, persistence of beliefs, persistence of affective capacities, and the like, are largely unaffected by self-transformation. And since self-transformation involves a reranking, not a replacement, of an agent's initial preferences, it preserves most of the two-place preference relations comprising an agent's preference set. For these reasons, transformed agents will be highly continuous with their untransformed selves, at least in the absence of independent disruptions to their psychological continuity.

Nor does self-transformation entail a violation of the second of these requirements. Many of the causal connections linking the psychological states of a transformed contractor with her untransformed self are entirely unaffected by self-transformation. And those causal connections between states forged by self-transformation are instances of continuity caused in the right way. For on self-transformation, an agent revises her preferences through a voluntary course of habituation which decomposes fully into a set of normal psychological processes.[53] Nothing could be further from the unwelcome changes to an agent's preferences caused by such disruptions of her normal psychological processes as brainwashing, neurological tampering, or unsolicited hypnosis.

Thus, self-transformation no more entails a loss of identity on the third of the above accounts of personal identity than it does on the first two. And thus, the objection to self-transformation based on the worry that agents could not survive it is ill-founded.

Conclusion

In this chapter, we have described self-transformation, compared it to previous attempts to establish that rational agents would act justly rather than unjustly for the right reason, argued that it avoids problems plaguing these attempts and defended it against several objections. Next, we turn to showing that the contractors we have described, occupying the choice situation we have described, would choose self-transformation over their other options.

Notes

1. Weaker conditions of coherence have, however, been studied extensively. See, for example, Amartya Sen, *Collective Choice and Social Welfare* (San Francisco: Holden Day, Inc., 1970), 7–20.

2. These additional conditions are monotonicity, continuity, substitutability, and reduction of compound lotteries. For a discussion of these conditions, see R.

D. Luce and H. Raiffa, *Games and Decisions* (New York: John Wiley & Sons, Inc., 1957), Chapter 2.

3. We argue, in the next chapter, that our characterization of contractors and their choice situation implies that they would so order the possible outcomes of their interactions, at least initially.

4. For a detailed presentation of the *PD*, see Richmond Campbell, "Background for the Uninitiated," in *Paradoxes of Rationality and Cooperation*, ed. Richmond Campbell and Lanning Sowden (Vancouver: University of British Columbia Press, 1985), 3–41.

5. Strictly speaking, preferences relate states of affairs, not actions. But for brevity's sake, we shall sometimes use "a preference for acting justly rather than unjustly," and similar locutions, to mean "an agent's preference for outcomes in which she acts justly over outcomes in which she acts unjustly."

6. This tradition dates back at least to Glaucon's appeal to the myth of Gyges in the *Republic*. See Plato, *The Republic*, trans. G. M. A. Grube (Indianapolis: Hackett Publishing Co., 1992), 35–6.

7. For a detailed discussion of the relationship between morality and constraint, see Duncan MacIntosh, "Preference's Progress: Rational Self-Alteration and the Rationality of Morality," *Dialogue* 30 (1991): 11–3.

8. For a similar claim, see John Rawls, *A Theory of Justice* (Cambridge: Harvard University Press, 1971), 46.

9. For a detailed discussion on the conditions under which it is rational to reconsider revised preferences, see Duncan MacIntosh, "Persons and the Satisfaction of Preferences: Problems in the Rational Kinematics of Value," *Journal of Philosophy* 90 (1993): 163–80.

10. See Amartya Sen, "Choice, Orderings, and Morality," in *Practical Reasoning*, ed. Stephan Korner (Oxford: Basil Blackwell Press, 1974), 54–67.

11. In discussing Sen's proposal, we let C = cooperate and D = defect. Otherwise, our conventions for representing preference orderings are the same as above.

12. For the analysis of Sen's proposal which follows, I am indebted to Duncan MacIntosh. See Duncan MacIntosh, "Co-operative Solutions to the Prisoner's Dilemma," *Philosophical Studies* 64 (1991): 313–6.

13. But perhaps an agent who chooses as if she had *AG* or *OR* preferences would enjoy more opportunities for cooperation than an agent who chooses as if she had *PD* preferences. And perhaps as a result of this increase, the former disposition would pay more than the latter disposition, so that rationality would require agents with *PD* preferences to act as if they had acquired *AG* or *OR* preferences. This is Gauthier's insight. We evaluate it in the next section.

14. For a treatment of constrained maximization, see David Gauthier, *Morals By Agreement* (New York: Oxford University Press, 1986), 157–89. For a treatment of the sense of justice, see David Gauthier, "Value, Reasons, and the Sense of Justice," in *Value, Welfare, and Morality*, ed. R. G. Frey and Christopher Morris (Cambridge: Cambridge University Press, 1993), 180–208.

15. See Alan Nelson, "Economic Rationality and Morality," *Philosophy and Public Affairs* 17 (1988): 160.

16. See Peter Danielson, *Artificial Morality: Virtuous Robots for Virtual Games* (London: Routledge, 1992), 157–62.

17. See Robert Frank, *Passions Within Reason* (New York: W. W. Norton and Co., 1988), Chapter 3.

18. See Gregory S. Kavka, review of *Morals by Agreement*, *Mind* 96 (1987): 117–21. See also Mark Vorabej, "Gauthier on Deterrence," *Dialogue* 25 (1986): 471–6.

19. See MacIntosh, "Co-operative Solutions," 311–2.

20. This reading of constrained maximization is Duncan MacIntosh's. See MacIntosh, "Preference's Progress," 11–2.

21. See Gauthier, "Value," 202.

22. For this account, see E. F. McClennen, *Rationality and Dynamic Choice: Foundational Explorations* (Cambridge: Cambridge University Press, 1990). In describing McClennen's account, I have drawn heavily on Gauthier's reconstruction of it in his unpublished "Resolute Choice and Rational Deliberation: A Critique and a Defence."

23. See McClennen, 113.

24. For several other such problems, see McClennen, 183–99.

25. This choice problem has been widely discussed in the literature. See, for instance, John Elster, *Ulysses and the Sirens* (Cambridge: Cambridge University Press, 1979), 36–111.

26. I have adapted this perspicuous representation of the major theories of personal identity from one offered by Duncan MacIntosh. See MacIntosh, "Persons and the Satisfaction of Preferences," 177. I have, however, substituted a version of the brain theory for the version of the body theory in MacIntosh's representation. For an argument that the most plausible physical criterion of personal identity involves continuity of the brain, not of the entire body, see Derek Parfit, *Reasons and Persons* (Oxford: Clarendon Press, 1984), 202–4.

27. For a discussion of the first account's failings, see Parfit, 223–8. For difficulties with the second, see Parfit, 253–70. And for objections to the third, see Bernard Williams, "Persons, Character, and Morality," in *The Identities of Persons*, ed. Amelie Oksenberg Rorty (Berkeley: University of California Press, 1976), 201–10.

28. For this argument, see McClennen, 183–99.

29. For a choice problem in which a myopic chooser would select a plan dominated with respect to sure outcomes by the plan a resolute chooser would select, see McClennen, 184–90.

30. For a choice problem in which a sophisticated chooser would select a plan dominated with respect to sure outcomes by the plan a resolute chooser would select, see McClennen, 190–5.

31. Some think that this argument fails. See, for instance, Duncan MacIntosh, "McClennen's Early Co-operative Solution to the Prisoner's Dilemma," *The Southern Journal of Philosophy* 39 (1991): 341–58. See also John Broome, review of *Rationality and Dynamic Choice: Foundational Explorations, Ethics* 102 (1992): 666–8.

32. For an argument to this effect, see McClennen, pp. 207–8.

33. See George Ainslie, "Specious Reward: A Behavioral Theory of Impulsiveness and Impulse Control," *Psychological Bulletin* 82 (1975): 463–96.

34. See Michael Bratman, *Intention, Plans, and Practical Reason* (Cambridge: Harvard University Press, 1987).

35. I learned this objection from E. F. McClennen. See McClennen, pp. 208–9.

36. Bruno Verbeek expresses just this worry about such a defense of *SEP* his unpublished "On the Rationality of Intentions."

37. Duncan MacIntosh develops his proposal over a series of articles. See, for instance, Duncan MacIntosh, "Two Gauthiers?" *Dialogue* 28 (1989): 43–61. Or see MacIntosh, "Preference's Progress." Or see MacIntosh, "Co-operative Solutions."

38. Described in this way, one might think that MacIntosh's proposal does not differ significantly from McClennen's. But MacIntosh's agents, unlike resolute choosers, follow *SEP* rather than *NEC* in cases of conflict between the two principles.

39. See MacIntosh, "Preference's Progress," 15.

40. See MacIntosh, "Persons and the Satisfaction of Preferences," 165. See also Duncan MacIntosh, "Preference-Revision and the Paradoxes of Instrumental Rationality," *Canadian Journal of Philosophy* 22 (1992): 519–20.

41. See Danielson.

42. Where acquiring information about the strategies of others involves costs, things are not nearly so neat. See Danielson, 148–62.

43. See Danielson, 129–47.

44. Peter Danielson realizes this, of course. Within the context of his project, it is not a worry. Within the context of mine, it is.

45. Peter Danielson recognizes this, and argues that artificial morality is nonetheless acceptable, because it closes the gap between rationality and morality no less effectively than its closest competitor, constrained maximization. See Danielson, 111–23. But this does not help it against self-transformation, which closes this gap more effectively than either.

46. I learned this objection, and an answer to it, from Duncan MacIntosh. See MacIntosh, "Preference-Revision," 507.

47. Duncan MacIntosh raises this objection in defending his account of preference revision. See Duncan MacIntosh, "Retaliation Rationalized: Gauthier's Solution to the Deterrence Dilemma," *Pacific Philosophical Quarterly* 72 (1991): 9–32. I have added nothing significant to his treatment of it.

48. I learned this worry from Duncan MacIntosh as well. See Duncan MacIntosh, "Persons and the Satisfaction of Preferences," 171–3.

49. For a defense of instrumentalism against several alternatives, see MacIntosh, "Persons and the Satisfaction of Preferences."

50. For a similar point, see MacIntosh, "Preference-Revision," 517.

51. Duncan MacIntosh raises this objection in defending his account of preference revision. See MacIntosh, "Persons and the Satisfaction of Preferences," 177–80. My answer to it owes much to MacIntosh's.

52. See Parfit, 206–9. As Derek Parfit notes, this is only a criterion of personal identity in non-branching cases.

53. For this decomposition, see Chapter 9.

4

The Collective Rationality of Self-Transformation

If each of our contractors would satisfy her preferences more fully if most or all transformed themselves than if most or all did not, then self-transformation is *collectively rational* for them. And if each would satisfy her preferences more fully if she transformed herself than if she did not, then self-transformation is *individually rational* for them. Within the justificatory framework we have developed, we provide members of our community with a fundamental justification of the sense of justice by showing that self-transformation is both collectively and individually rational for our contractors. I shall argue for the collective rationality of self-transformation in this chapter, and for its individual rationality over the next several chapters.

The choice situation we have defined involves two stages. At the first stage, contractors agree upon a joint strategy for implementing rules of justice, and take whatever measures are required to insure that they can execute this strategy successfully. At the second stage, they choose individual strategies for satisfying their preferences within the context created by their actions at the first stage. We establish the collective rationality of self-transformation by showing that at the first stage of their choice situation, contractors would choose a joint strategy requiring most or all of them to transform themselves.

Instrumentally Rational Choice Among Joint Strategies

In a community like our own, rules of justice specify the proportion of its cooperative output received by each of its members. Each can increase her share of this output by increasing the size of this output. And as shares of this output increase, each can satisfy her preferences more fully. Indeed, choosing a joint strategy for implementing rules of justice in the absence of individual strategies for satisfying their preferences under such rules, contractors can increase their individual utility payoffs in no other way.

In determining what joint strategy for implementing rules of justice contractors would choose, we shall assume that they follow one of the decision rules among which the decision value framework arbitrates, the expected utility principle. By so doing, we simplify our analysis of choice at the first stage of contractors' choice situation. And besides, at this stage, contractors would choose in the same manner were they maximizing expected utility or maximizing decision value.[1] In light of the above considerations, this translates into the assumption that contractors would agree upon the joint strategy expected to maximize their net cooperative output.

Some Assumptions of Our Analysis

In arguing for the collective rationality of self-transformation, we invoke a number of assumptions, detailed below. We rely upon these in arguing for the individual rationality of self-transformation as well, although we supplement them with a number of other assumptions.

First, we assume that contractors engage in rounds of interaction. Each round consists of simultaneous interactions between pairs of contractors lasting a year.[2] Our interaction surely has a less regular structure than this. But so conceiving of interaction among contractors renders it easier to model, and does not alter significantly any of the interaction problems with which we shall concern ourselves.

Second, we assume that contractors do not know the upper bound on the number of such rounds in which members of their community will participate. But we also assume that contractors are mortal, like us. This insures that although interaction between contractors is open-ended, each can participate in but a finite number of rounds. And lacking foreknowledge of the times of their own deaths, no contractor can determine the precise number of rounds in which she will participate. By so conceiving of contractors, we capture our own expectations about the persistence of social cooperation, and about the roles we each play within it.

Third, we assume that contractors inhabit a community characterized by zero population growth. In particular, we assume that any contractors removed from interaction are replaced by a like number of contractors, through immigration and the maturation of the offspring of present contractors. Again, this assumption distorts our own circumstances somewhat, but not in a way which alters the interaction problems we shall consider. It is, thus, a permissible simplifying assumption.

Fourth, we assume that the more injustice occurring among contractors, the smaller their cooperative output. The more injustice occurring among contractors, the more they will fear being victimized by their fellows. The more they fear such victimization, the less contractors will cooperate with one another. And the less contractors cooperate with one another, the smaller their cooperative output will be. Thus, we are justified in assuming that injustice is collectively costly.

Fifth, we assume that absent an enforcement mechanism, acting justly pays a contractor less than acting unjustly during any given interaction. Did injustice not pay more than justice, contractors would not find themselves in the partial conflict of interests characterizing the circumstances of justice.

Sixth, and finally, we assume that on any given interaction, the payoff for acting justly is smaller, in absolute terms, than the cost of being exploited by someone who acts unjustly. For her part in a given cooperative interaction, each contractor realizes the following net payoff: a share of its gross yield (x) minus her contribution (y) to it, or $x-y$. Having been exploited during a given interaction, a contractor realizes no share of its gross yield, and loses her contribution to it, for a net payoff of $-y$. Under the circumstances of justice, both x and y are positive, and $x > y$, so that $-y < x-y$. Thus, our assumption that being exploited costs one of our contractors more than she stands to gain by acting justly is justified.

A Decision Problem

Consider the set of all rounds in which the members of a community participate over its lifetime. Let us define a *representative round* as the member of this set we would be most likely to select were we selecting from this set at random. Given that contractors would engage in an indefinitely large number of rounds whatever their choice of joint strategies, as we have assumed, we can determine how they would choose at the first stage of their choice situation by determining how they would choose during a representative round were they choosing a joint strategy for implementing rules of justice during such a round.

Drawing upon the above assumptions, we shall model the latter choice as a decision problem. To describe this decision problem fully, we must specify its player set, its strategy set, and its payoff function. The player set of this decision problem consists of all of our contractors. To specify its strategy set and payoff function, we must examine the structure of their interaction in more detail.

The PD Involved in Complying with Rules of Justice

In any given pairwise interaction, each contractor may cooperate by acting justly or defect by acting unjustly.[3] Thus, each interacting pair will realize one of four possible outcomes: the first defects while the second cooperates (*DC*), both cooperate (*CC*), both defect (*DD*), the first cooperates while the second defects (*CD*).

Each ranks first the outcome in which she defects and her partner cooperates, since exploitation pays. Each ranks second the outcome in which both cooperate. On this outcome, both realize a share of the benefits produced by their mutually beneficial cooperation. Each ranks third the outcome in which both defect. On this outcome, mutually beneficial cooperation does not occur, since neither complies with the rules of justice defining the terms of such cooperation. But given that contractors can only be exploited when acting justly, neither is exploited by the other. Each ranks last the outcome in which she cooperates and her partner defects, since being exploited is costly. This ordering of outcomes—*DC*, *CC*, *DD*, *CD*—defines the standard prisoner's dilemma (*PD*), represented in Figure 4.1.

The *PD* is really two problems.[4] First, even were each party to the *PD* willing to cooperate were her partner to cooperate as well, defecting would yield her third-ranked rather than her fourth-ranked outcome were her partner to defect. Thus, without some assurance that her partner will cooperate, each has an incentive to defect. Call this the *assurance problem*.[5] And second, were her partner to cooperate, defecting would yield each party to the PD her first-ranked rather than her second-ranked outcome. Thus, even assured that her partner will cooperate, each has an incentive to defect. Call this the *free-rider problem*. In the face of these two problems, defection dominates cooperation for parties to the *PD*, so rational ones would defect.[6]

Proposed Solutions to the PD

To implement rules of justice, contractors must resolve the *PD* involved in complying with such rules. Several resolutions to the *PD* have been proposed.[7] We shall examine each of these, rejecting those which have no significance within the context of our project. From the solutions remaining, we shall construct a strategy set for contractors' decision problem.

The Symmetry Solution.   According to the symmetry solution, since equally rational agents would choose similarly in similar situations, and since each party to the *PD* does better if both cooperate than if both defect, each would choose to cooperate in the *PD*.[8] But while both parties to the *PD* do better if both cooperate than if both defect, each does better for herself no matter what the other does by defecting. Since our contractors are maximizers, each would always seek to do as well for herself as possible, so each would defect in the *PD*. Thus, the symmetry solution is not available to our contractors.

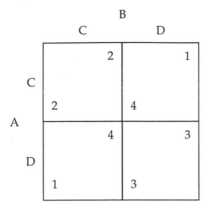

Figure 4.1   The *PD*, with Agent *A*'s Preference Ranking over Outcomes in the Bottom Left Corners, and Agent *B*'s in the Top Right Corners, of Each Square

Alternative Principle Solutions.   Alternative principle solutions revise the theory of rational choice. They do not simply recommend that agents follow a different decision rule as a means to instrumentally rational choice. Rather, they recommend a revision in this theory of rationality itself.[9]

Such solutions cannot help our contractors resolve their *PD*, for as we have argued, we best serve our project by conceiving of them as instrumentally rational. Hence, how agents rational in some other sense might be able to resolve the *PD* has no bearing on the predicament of our contractors.

Resolution Solutions.   In resolution solutions, an agent resolves to cooperate in the *PD* against her exogenously specified preferences because she realizes that there are pragmatic benefits to doing so. Having so resolved, her preferences change endogenously, so that she prefers to follow through on her resolution to cooperate in the *PD*.[10]

Resolution solutions are available only to agents whose preferences respond directly, spontaneously, and automatically to rational criticism. But our contractors are not such agents. Thus, resolution solutions are not available to our contractors.

Mechanism Solutions.   In mechanism solutions, agents set up some mechanism to insure that they will cooperate in the *PD* against their preferences. They might, for instance, take a pill causing them to cooperate. Alternatively, they might program a machine to cooperate for them. Or they might condition themselves to cooperate whatever their preferences might be.

It might be rational for agents to set up some such mechanism in some *PD*s. But an individual who has delegated to a mechanism the decision to cooperate in the *PD* no longer acts rationally in so cooperating. Indeed, she no longer acts at all.

Actions are caused by reasons which rationalize them, analyzed into complexes of beliefs and preferences within the framework we have presupposed. But the behavior of an individual who has delegated her decision to a mechanism is not caused by any such complex. Rather, it is caused by a mechanism which bypasses her beliefs and preferences entirely. And behavior which is not caused by reasons rationalizing it is not action.[11]

But perhaps behavior caused by a mechanism is action under certain conditions, when the mechanism itself is rationalized by the appropriate complex of beliefs and preferences within the agent whose behavior it determines. This may be, but it is of no help in establishing that cooperative behavior in the *PD* caused by a mechanism is action. For in the *PD*, each individual's beliefs and preferences support defection, not cooperation. And surely behavior which is neither caused by reasons, nor rationalized by them, is not action.

That mechanism solutions undercut the capacity of individuals for action does not imply that such solutions are irrational. But we seek to establish that instrumental rationality requires individuals like us to maintain the sense of justice. Since individuals caused to behave justly rather than unjustly by a mechanism do not act justly rather than unjustly, they cannot exhibit a disposition to act justly rather than unjustly. Thus, an appeal to mechanism solutions to the *PD* involved in complying with rules of justice can reveal nothing about whether rationality requires individuals like us to maintain the sense of justice. And thus, within the context of our project, such solutions have no significance.

Preference Revision Solutions.   In preference revision solutions, agents revise those of their preferences responsible for their defecting rather than cooperating in the *PD*. Then they choose among actions based on their revised preferences.

But if contractors attempted a preference revision solution to the *PD* involved in acting justly rather than unjustly, they would find themselves in a higher-order *PD*. Attempting such a solution, contractors must choose between retaining their *PD* preferences and revising them. But all of the incentives for contractors to defect in their original *PD* are equally incentives for them to retain their *PD* preferences, since just these cause them to defect in their original *PD*. Thus, contractors seeking a preference revision solution to their original *PD* confront an equivalent *PD* in revising their *PD* preferences. And choosing rationally in this *PD*, contractors would retain their *PD* preferences, failing to resolve their original *PD*.

Perhaps contractors could resolve this preference revision *PD* by means of an agreement. But contractors would keep an agreement to revise their *PD* preferences just in case they could expect to maximize over these preferences by doing so. And if such preference revision involves the higher-order *PD* we have described, then violating an agreement to revise their *PD* preferences would dominate keeping such an agreement for contractors. Choosing rationally, contractors would violate an agreement to revise their *PD* preferences.

An *assurance contract* is an agreement to contribute to a collectively rational outcome incorporating a refund feature.[12] The members of a community could use assurance contracts to resolve the *PD*s associated with producing public goods.[13] By refunding contributions to a public good in the event of insufficient participation in its production, they could assure one another of the safety of making such contributions. And by requiring unanimous contribution to a public good as a condition of its production, they could render free-riding on the contributions of others to this good impossible. If each member of a community valued her share of a public good more than her share of the costs of producing it, then she would pay her share of these costs in the context of such an assurance contract.[14]

Each of our contractors might agree to revise her *PD* preferences just in case all others do so as well, with the costs of preference revision being refunded to those who have revised their preferences if any fail to do so. And one might think that by means of such an agreement, contractors could resolve their preference revision *PD*.

But such an agreement could not alleviate the free-rider component of this *PD*. Think of the widespread possession of the sense of justice within a community as a public good.[15] Because contractors are opaque, they cannot determine whether this public good has been produced prior to interacting with one another. And by the time they interact with one another, contractors have already produced this public good, if they are going to produce it at all. Thus, contractors cannot prevent individuals from free-riding on the preference revision of others by making the enjoyment of the public good constituted by widespread possession of the sense of justice conditional upon unanimous preference revision.

It might seem that contractors could alleviate this free-rider problem by agreeing to reacquire their *PD* preferences if any of them retained their *PD* preferences. But given the costs involved in preference revision, rational contractors would not keep such an agreement unless a substantial number of them retained their *PD* preferences. Thus, free-riding remains an option for contractors who have so agreed. Indeed, for such contractors, the choice of whether or not to free-ride itself constitutes a *PD*, with free-riding the dominant move. And finding themselves in this *PD*, our contractors would all retain their *PD* preferences, failing to resolve the *PD* involved in revising these preferences.

This does not imply, however, that preference revision can play no part in a successful resolution of the *PD* involved in complying with rules of justice. As we shall see, conjoined to a particular inducement solution, preference revision enables contractors to resolve this *PD*.

Inducement Solutions. Inducement solutions involve agents altering their circumstances so that doing something previously dispreferred is advantageous. If they made cooperation rewarding enough, or defection costly enough, then their interaction would no longer have the structure of the *PD*. They would cooperate to secure the reward associated with co-operation or to avoid the penalty associated with defection.

Let us distinguish between negative inducement solutions, which penalize defection, and positive inducement solutions, which reward cooperation. Whether contractors penalize defection or reward cooperation, they must monitor their interactions, and administer penalties or rewards. Let us assume that monitoring costs would be equal on both negative and positive inducement solutions to the *PD* involved in acting justly rather than unjustly. And let us assume that punishing defection would cost contractors no less than rewarding cooperation, even though a deterrent effect would almost certainly render the former less costly than the latter among contractors resembling us. Even given these two assumptions, our contractors would opt for negative inducement solutions to their *PD* over positive inducement solutions to it, for the following reason.

Rewarding contractors for acting justly rather than unjustly provides them with an incentive to cooperate as much as they can with others, even in some cases where cooperation is counterproductive. And operating under such an incentive structure, their cooperation would tend to be less efficient than it would otherwise be. Thus, given the above assumptions, rewarding compliance with rules of justice would yield contractors a smaller net cooperative output than punishing violations of such rules.

One might think that contractors could remedy this defect of positive inducement solutions by rewarding only just actions occurring in the context of efficient cooperation. But to do so, they would have to monitor not only their compliance with rules of justice, but also the efficiency of their particular cooperative interactions. Since the resources to support this additional monitoring must come from somewhere, such a solution to their *PD* would still yield contractors a smaller net cooperative output than would a negative inducement solution to it, at least given the above assumptions.

And so, even if positive and negative inducement solutions are equally capable of resolving the *PD* involved in complying with rules of justice, contractors would opt for the latter over the former. For by doing so, they could expect to maximize their net cooperative output. Thus, in considering inducement solutions to this *PD*, we can restrict ourselves to negative ones.

Let an *enforcement mechanism* be the subset of a community empowered to detect, apprehend, judge, and penalize those violating its rules of justice. Within the class of negative inducement solutions to the *PD* involved in complying with rules of justice, we shall restrict our attention to those deploying an enforcement mechanism resembling our own.

We can, of course, conceive of other negative inducement solutions to this *PD*.[16] But we shall disregard these. Some are technologically remote from our own circumstances, and thus of little interest within the context of our project. And those less remote technologically from our own circumstances are nonetheless politically remote, in that they constitute what many would regard as an unacceptable compromising of political ideals. If we wish our contractors to stand proxy for us, we should restrict their options to those we can and would implement.

To resolve the *PD* involved in acting justly rather than unjustly, contractors might attach a penalty of f to some proportion, say $1-z$, of all violations of rules of justice occurring each round. Under such an enforcement mechanism, each contractor's odds of being punished for any particular violation would be $1-z$, and these odds would vary with the value of z. To alleviate their free-rider and assurance problems, contractors need only keep $1-z$ high enough that, when conjoined with an appropriate f, the expected payoff of acting justly is larger than that of acting unjustly.

One might worry, however, that among opaque contractors, an enforcement mechanism could not identify penalties capable of dissuading contractors from free-riding.[17] And without at least one such penalty at its disposal, an enforcement mechanism could alleviate neither the free-rider nor the assurance problem involved in complying with rules of justice.

But that contractors have at least one such penalty at their disposal follows from their occupying the circumstances of justice. In the circumstances of justice, contractors cannot satisfy their preferences as fully working alone as they can by cooperating. And each, by assumption, wishes to satisfy her preferences as fully as possible. Thus, there is a penalty all of our contractors would be anxious to avoid—exclusion from beneficial social cooperation.

By excluding those violating rules of justice from cooperation just long enough for their losses from exclusion to exceed their gains from acting unjustly, contractors could alleviate their free-rider problem. So penalizing violators might not be enough to alleviate their assurance problem, however, for the following reasons.

The flaws of some dispose them to violate offensively, so as to exploit others, even when their prospects of getting away with doing so are dim. By violating offensively under such conditions, such contractors reveal flaws severe enough to undermine their capacity for choosing rationally, at least when it comes to restraining their predatory urges. And reintroducing such contractors into social cooperation after they have been excluded would make the less flawed nervous about acting justly rather than unjustly in the future.

The flaws of others dispose them to violate defensively, so as to avoid being exploited themselves, upon very little provocation. Those most flawed in this respect might violate rules of justice defensively in response to the reintroduction of their predatory fellows into cooperation. The reintroduction of these defensive violators into social cooperation would make contractors nervous about acting justly rather than unjustly. In this climate, the slightly less flawed might violate defensively. The subsequent reintroduction of these into cooperation would make contractors more nervous yet. This might lead to further violations by those even less flawed, and so on, until so many were acting unjustly that rationality would require all to violate defensively. Such a spiral would culminate in the complete breakdown in compliance with rules of justice.

Among contractors with certain distributions of flaws, excluding violators from cooperation temporarily would yield a spiral towards injustice. And since the distribution of flaws among individuals may shift over time, a community that so penalized violators would be vulnerable always to a complete breakdown in compliance with rules of justice. Thus, were they to exclude violators from cooperation temporarily, contractors might fail to alleviate the assurance problem involved in acting justly rather than unjustly.

Things would be different, however, were contractors to exclude violators from cooperation permanently.[18] This penalty is high enough to capture contractors' attention, perhaps dissuading some potential violators from their course. Further, by so penalizing violators, contractors would assuage the worries of the less flawed about being exploited by the more flawed. And because permanent exclusion from cooperation is a disaster on a par with being exploited, so penalizing violators would dissuade the less flawed from violating defensively even in the face of widespread violations by the more flawed. Thus, by means of this penalty, contractors could prevent the less flawed from emulating violations by the more flawed, alleviating their assurance problem no matter what the distribution of flaws among them.

Although we have imagined that contractors would punish some proportion of the violations occurring each round, one might think they could be more discriminating, punishing only offensive violations, and still resolve the *PD* involved in complying with rules of justice. In the absence of a perfectly effective enforcement mechanism, however, contractors are always at risk of being victimized by an offensive violator. Awareness of this possibility might induce the most flawed to violate rules of justice defensively. Such violations would make contractors more nervous, perhaps inducing the slightly less flawed to violate defensively, and so on, yielding the same spiral of violations described above. To prevent such a spiral, contractors must dissuade those capable of fully rational action from violating defensively. And punishing only offensive violators would accomplish nothing in this regard.

As we have described the enforcement mechanism implemented by contractors, it is composed of opaque contractors. But could contractors not determine the dispositions of their fellows, one might think, they could not determine whether their enforcement mechanism would enforce effectively prior to its operation. And absent this information, one might object, contractors could not empower an enforcement mechanism capable of resolving the *PD* involved in acting justly rather than unjustly from within their choice situation.

Contractors must take one another as they find one another, but they design their enforcement mechanism. And they can design it so as to insure its effectiveness. Although contractors are opaque, they know that all desire a share of their cooperative output. And they can use some of this output to create incentives for serving within their enforcement mechanism. By making these incentives large enough, and by making payment of them conditional upon the effective performance of the tasks involved in enforcing rules of justice, contractors can induce their rational fellows to perform these tasks, even knowing nothing of their dispositions. Thus, an enforcement mechanism constructed out of opaque contractors need not itself be opaque to contractors.

One might yet worry that permanent exclusion from cooperation is so harsh a penalty as to cause us to reject the circumstances of contractors as representative of our own. But this worry is vain. For we have focused on violations among contractors resulting in disastrous consequences for those exploited. And in our community, we punish such violations very harshly indeed, imposing penalties ranging from extended imprisonment to death. Thus, rather than alienating us, the harsh penalty contractors impose upon violators should make it easier for us to identify with them.

There are surely other enforcement technologies capable of resolving the *PD* involved in acting justly rather than unjustly. For our purposes, however, what matters is not how opaque contractors would resolve this, but that they could do so whatever the distribution of flaws among them. Hence, rather than arguing that a particular enforcement technology is optimal for contractors, we shall simply assume that they punish 1–z of the violations occurring each round by excluding both offensive and defensive violators from cooperation permanently.

A Short List of Strategies

Having rejected four of the six proposed solutions to the *PD* as unsuitable for our purposes, we shall generate a short list of joint strategies available to contractors for putting their designated conception of justice into practice. On this list, we shall include two strategies, one representative of inducement solutions to the *PD*, the other a combination of preference revision and inducement solutions to the *PD*. The two strategies on this list comprise the strategy set for contractors' decision problem.

On the *policer* strategy, contractors empower an enforcement mechanism to induce one another to act justly rather than unjustly. They exclude some proportion of those violating rules of justice offensively and defensively each round from all future cooperation, a proportion just high enough to decrease the expected payoff of acting unjustly below that of acting justly.

On the *policed transformer* strategy (the *transformer* strategy, for short), contractors empower an enforcement mechanism to induce most members of their community to transform themselves, and then most of them transform themselves. Since our contractors are opaque, an enforcement mechanism cannot detect their dispositions directly and punish those who do not develop principled preferences. But by permanently excluding a large enough proportion of offensive and defensive violators from interaction each round, an enforcement mechanism can decrease the payoff of retaining *PD* preferences below that of developing principled preferences for most of our contractors. Or so I shall argue.

There are other means of implementing rules of justice than the policer and transformer strategies. But we have to restrict the strategy set of contractors' decision problem enough to make it tractable. And the policer and transformer strategies are representative of solutions to the *PD* with a special significance for us, given our project. On these grounds, we shall restrict the strategy set of contractors' decision problem to the entries on our short list of strategies. Given this restriction, and our previous assumptions, showing that contractors would choose a joint strategy requiring self-transformation at the first stage of their choice situation reduces to showing that within this decision problem, they would choose the true transformer over the policer strategy.

This way of proceeding is less than ideal, for it requires us to conditionalize our conclusions on the adequacy of our short list. There is some consolation, however, in realizing that we can always update our argument by making additions to this list, if and when more promising solutions to the *PD* involved in acting justly rather than unjustly become available.

A Payoff Function

Having already characterized the player and strategy sets of contractors' decision problem, we turn to specifying the components of its payoff function.

Define *trust* as the expectation that others will act justly even when they are not likely to be penalized for acting unjustly. Contractors who do not trust one another cooperate only when they expect their enforcement mechanism to be sufficiently effective. Contractors who trust one another, contrastingly, cooperate in all such situations, and then some. Thus, trust effectively extends the range of situations under which contractors cooperate. By so doing, it increases productive cooperation among contractors, and thus, their cooperative output.

Policers have no grounds for trusting one another. Transformers, however, would trust one another if enough of them developed principled preferences. Let b represent contractors' *base cooperative output*, what policers would gross from any given round's interaction, and what transformers would gross from any given round's interaction did they fail to transform themselves. Let s represent the increase in their cooperative output during any given round transformers would realize as the result of self-transformation.

Let c represent the proportion of b policers spend each round to maintain an enforcement mechanism capable of resolving the *PD* involved in acting justly rather than unjustly. Let x and y represent the proportions of b that policers and transformers, respectively, spend *in toto* punishing each violation of rules of justice.[19]

As we shall see, transformers typically require a more responsive and effective mechanism than the one c would purchase. So let d represent the proportion of b transformers spend each round over and above c to enhance their enforcement mechanism's responsiveness.[20] And let e represent the proportion of b transformers spend each round over and above c to enhance its effectiveness.

Let v and w represent the number of violations occurring during any given round per hundred policers and transformers, respectively. Let $1-o$

and $1-p$ represent the proportion of violations punished during any given round by policer and transformer enforcement mechanisms, respectively.

We can define the payoff function of contractors' decision problem in terms of these variables. Broadly speaking, we calculate the payoffs of the policer (P) and transformer (T) strategies during any given round by subtracting the costs of each from its benefits. The payoff to the set of all contractors (N) on each of these strategies during any given round is described by the following function:

$$U_N(P) = b - (cb + (1{-}o)(v/100)Nxb)$$

$$U_N(T) = (b{+}sb) - [(cb + db + eb) + (1{-}p)(w/100)Nyb]$$

Because we have assumed that policers and transformers would operate with the same enforcement technology, we represent them as paying the same base enforcement cost each round, cb. Since transformers typically maintain a more responsive and more effective enforcement mechanism than policers, we represent them as paying enforcement costs each round policers do not pay, db and eb. As suggested by our discussion of mutual trust, we represent this investment as paying off in a cooperative increase for transformers each round policers do not realize, sb. Because they purchase differing amounts of enforcement effectiveness, we represent policers and transformers as punishing different proportions of the violations committed each round, $1-o$ as compared to $1-p$. As they punish different proportions of the violations committed each round, we represent policers and transformers as having to contend with different numbers of violations each round, $(v/100)N$ as compared to $(w/100)N$. And finally, because they punish different numbers of violations each round, we represent policers and transformers as spending different total amounts on each violation they must punish, xb as compared to yb.

One might worry that this payoff function is incomplete. Transformers, as we shall describe them, develop principled preferences through habituation. And to do so, each must initially expend time and effort that individual policers need not expend. If policers invested the time and effort they would have spent transforming themselves in cooperation, they could increase their initial cooperative output. And if they reinvested this initial cooperative increase in cooperation, they could increase their future cooperative output as well. By disregarding the costs of adopting the policer and transformer strategies, we suppress this possibility. And by suppressing this possibility, one might object, we privilege the transformer over the policer strategy, contrary to the demands of our project.

But the policer strategy involves its own characteristic costs, costs transformers avoid. If she is to avoid punishment for violating rules of justice, a policer must conceal her violations from others. Indeed, under an enforcement mechanism which punishes a set proportion of the violations occurring each round, a policer must conceal any violation she commits more effectively than most of her fellow violators do. Thus, to survive and flourish under her community's enforcement mechanism, a policer must develop effective habits of concealment. Since developing such habits should cost contractors no less than developing habits of justice, we do not privilege the transformer over the policer strategy by disregarding the costs involved in adopting these strategies.

Payoff Parameters

To solve contractors' decision problem, we must compare the payoffs of the policer and transformer strategies during a representative round. To compare these payoffs, however, we must assign values to the terms comprising them. The values we assign to these terms must satisfy two conditions. First, because we seek to justify the sense of justice to members of our community, these values must reflect, or at least suggest, conditions within our own community. And second, because we are arguing for the collective rationality of the transformer over the policer strategy, we must specify these values to favor the latter over the former as much as the above condition permits. If contractors would choose the transformer over the policer strategy in this variant of their decision problem, then they would do so in variants less favorable to the policer strategy as well. Hence, to show that contractors would choose the transformer over the policer strategy in all variants of their decision problem suggestive of conditions within our own community, we need only show that they would do so in a variant satisfying the above two conditions.

The Value of **N.** N represents the membership of the set of all contractors. We want the payoff parameters of contractors' decision problem to reflect conditions within our own very large community. As N increases, however, so do the enforcement savings transformers realize over policers, increasing the payoff of the transformer strategy relative to that of the policer strategy. Seeking to favor the policer over the transformer strategy, we shall suppose that $N = 100,000$, much lower than the membership of our own community, but high enough to suggest its impersonal ambiance.

The Values of **v** *and* **w.**   By examining the types of mistakes that can cause contractors to violate rules of justice, we can learn something about the values of v and w, which represent the number of violations committed during any given round among policers and transformers, respectively.

First, a contractor might err in applying rules of justice within a particular situation. Second, a contractor might apply rules of justice correctly, but overestimate what she stands to gain by acting unjustly. Third, a contractor might apply rules of justice correctly, but overestimate her risk of being exploited by her partner. And fourth, a contractor might apply rules of justice correctly, but underestimate her risk of being punished for violating these rules.

Errors of all of these types might cause untransformed contractors to violate rules of justice. But while misapplying rules of justice might cause a transformed contractor to behave unjustly, errors of the other three types above would not. And so, although transformed contractors are susceptible to errors of all of the above types, only errors of the first type might cause them to violate rules of justice.

Because self-transformation does nothing to diminish the limitations from which contractors suffer, we can assume that transformed and untransformed contractors would err with equal frequency. In the absence of evidence that errors of any one of the above types are more prevalent among us than errors of any of the others, we shall also assume that errors of each of these types would occur with equal frequency among contractors. Given these assumptions, we can conclude that errors would cause untransformed contractors to violate rules of justice four times as frequently as transformed contractors during any given round.

All violations committed by transformed contractors would result from errors. Some violations committed by untransformed contractors would result from errors, others from sound decisions. Conjoined with the above conclusion, these two claims imply that untransformed contractors would violate rules of justice at least four times as frequently as transformed contractors during any given round. The more frequently untransformed contractors would behave unjustly relative to transformed contractors, the lower the payoff of the policer strategy would be relative to that of the transformer strategy. Thus, in specifying v and w, we shall assume that untransformed contractors would violate rules of justice four times as frequently as transformed contractors during any given round.

Over time, the operation of a transformer enforcement mechanism would drive the number of untransformed agents within a transformer community down to $.25N$ and keep it there.[21] Thus, during a representative round of interaction among transformers, between 0 and .25 of them would lack principled preferences. The more untransformed contractors a transformer community contains, the higher the payoff of the policer strategy is relative to that of the transformer strategy. Thus, in specifying the values of v and w during a representative round, we shall assume that

.25 of transformers would lack principled preferences during such a round.

Transformers lacking principled preferences would violate rules of justice as frequently as policers. The remaining .75 of a transformer community, however, would behave unjustly .25 as frequently as policers. These claims imply that during a representative round,

$$w = .25v + (.75)(.25)v.$$

Simplifying this expression, we find that during such a round, $w = .44v$.

Given the aim of our project, we should set the values of v and w during a representative round high enough to reflect conditions within our community. Like our community, a transformer community contains mostly individuals who possess principled preferences, and some who do not. Within our community, the annual rate of serious crimes has fluctuated between 5 and 6 per 100 residents for the last ten years.[22] So as to reflect conditions within our community, we shall stipulate that during a representative round, $w = 5.5$. Given this stipulation, it follows that $v = 12.5$ during such a round.

Because we have relied on statistics based on reported crimes in specifying the value of w during a representative round, and because not all serious crimes occurring within our community are reported, this specification is conservative. And because we have set the proportional relationship between v and w during a representative round as low as our characterization of contractors allows, our specification of the value of v during a representative round is conservative as well. As v and w increase (assuming that the proportional relationship between the two remains constant), so does the enforcement savings the transformer strategy promises contractors over the policer strategy. Hence, by specifying the values of v and w during a representative round conservatively, we favor the policer over the transformer strategy.

The Value of 1–o.   Policers punish $1-o$ of the violations occurring within their community during any given round. To resolve the *PD* involved in complying with rules of justice within a policer community, policers must set $1-o$ high enough to make defecting in this *PD* less profitable for themselves than cooperating in it. To determine just how high policers must set $1-o$ to accomplish this end, we must know their payoffs for cooperation and defection in this *PD*.

In Chapter 7, we specify these payoffs for transformers. Let u represent the utility each associates with expending the resources she has available to invest in interaction on the satisfaction of her preferences. Given this specification of u, each would receive u utiles for cooperating.

For defecting without being punished for doing so, each would receive $2u$ utiles. For being punished or being exploited, each would receive $-u$ utiles. We have assumed, quite arbitrarily, that $u = 2$ utiles within a trusting community.[23]

With the same options as transformers, policers face the same schedule of payoffs as transformers. But not trusting one another, policers would interact less than transformers, so each would have fewer resources to invest in interaction than her transformer counterparts. Thus, the value of u would be smaller among policers than among transformers. For our purposes, precisely how much smaller u would be among policers than among transformers does not matter. Thus, analyzing interaction among policers, we can assign u any value we like smaller than 2 utiles. We shall assume, quite arbitrarily, that $u = 1$ utile among policers, so that cooperating pays each 1 utile, defecting pays each 2 utiles, and being punished or exploited pays each -1 utile.

Given this specification of the payoffs of cooperation and defection among policers, we can calculate the values of o and $1-o$ during a representative round as follows. To render defection less profitable for themselves than cooperation during such a round, policers must set $1-o$ high enough to insure that

$$o(2) + (1-o)(-1) < (.875)(1) + (.125)(-1).^{24}$$

Solving this inequality for o, we find that $o < .58$, and $1-o > .42$. Thus, to resolve the *PD* involved in complying with rules of justice during a representative round, policers must insure that $1-o > .42$ during such a round. Because an enforcement mechanism costs more to maintain the more effective it is, we shall assume that a policer enforcement mechanism would punish .43 of the violations committed during a representative round, that $1-o = .43$ during such a round.

The Value of 1–p.   Transformers punish $1-p$ of the violations committed within their community during any given round. To resolve the *PD* involved in acting justly rather than unjustly within a transformer community, transformers must set $1-p$ high enough to make defecting in this *PD* less profitable for themselves than cooperating in it. To determine just how high transformers must set $1-p$ to accomplish this end, we must know their payoffs for cooperating and defecting in this *PD*.

We specify these payoffs in Chapter 7. For cooperating with one of her fellows, each transformer would receive 2 utiles. For defecting without being punished for doing so, each would receive 4 utiles. For being punished or being exploited, each would receive -2 utiles.[25]

Given this specification of the payoffs of cooperation and defection among transformers, we can calculate the values of p and $1-p$ during a representative round as follows. To render defection less profitable for themselves than cooperation during such a round, transformers must set $1-p$ high enough to insure that

$$p(4) + (1-p)(-2) < (2)(.945) + (-2)(.055).^{26}$$

Solving this inequality for p, we find that $p < .63$, and $1-p > .37$. Thus, to resolve the *PD* involved in complying with rules of justice during a representative round, transformers must insure that $1-p > .38$ during such a round. Accordingly, we shall assume that a transformer enforcement mechanism would punish at least .38 of the violations committed during a representative round.

But a transformer enforcement mechanism must do more than resolve the *PD* involved in complying with rules of justice. It must also induce contractors to instantiate the transformer strategy by developing principled preferences.

A perfectly effective enforcement mechanism, one which punishes every violation occurring within a community, could accomplish this end. For since their flaws dispose contractors lacking principled preferences to violate more frequently than those who have them, a perfectly effective enforcement mechanism would pose a greater threat to the former than to the latter. But if contractors occupy circumstances resembling our own, maintaining such an enforcement mechanism would be prohibitively expensive.

A less expensive way to accomplish the same end would be to implement a *responsive* enforcement mechanism. Such an enforcement mechanism punishes more of the violations occurring within a community during a round the greater the proportion of fakers operating within that community. Let k represent the proportion of contractors lacking principled preferences during any given round. We shall assume that a transformer enforcement mechanism operates by punishing $.38 + .62k$ of the violations committed during any given round, that $1-p = .38 + .62k$. Such an enforcement mechanism would always punish .38 of the violations occurring within a community, as required to resolve the *PD* transformers face in complying with rules of justice. And it would punish more violations each round as the value of k increases, between .38 and 1 of these, depending on the value of k. During a representative round, $0 \leq k \leq .25$. But the larger the value of k, the more the policer strategy pays contractors relative to the transformer strategy. Thus, in specifying the value of $1-p$ in the context of our argument for the collective rationality of self-transformation, we shall assume that k = .25 during a representative round. Under this assumption, $1-p$ = .54 during such a round.

Over the next several chapters, I shall argue that the operation of just such a responsive enforcement mechanism would render developing principled preferences a better gamble for most of our contractors than not doing so, no matter how many of them would actually transform themselves. If successful, this argument reveals how rational contractors jointly choosing the transformer strategy could induce one another to transform without the prohibitive expense of maintaining a perfectly effective enforcement mechanism.

Not only must a transformer enforcement mechanism induce contractors jointly choosing the transformer strategy to develop principled preferences, it must also nurture trust among them. We shall assume that trust is a threshold phenomenon.[27] For trust to develop among individuals, they must believe that no more than a certain proportion of their fellows would exploit them. We shall also assume that bonds of trust are delicate, that individuals need not be exploited many times before becoming distrustful. For trust to persist among individuals, they must correctly believe that no more than a certain proportion of their fellows would exploit them.[28]

Let us designate the maximum proportion of exploitative members a community can contain and still sustain trust as M. The higher M is, the more effective a transformer enforcement mechanism must be to nurture trust, and the harder it is to establish the collective rationality of self-transformation. Experience suggests that M is closer to 0 than to 1, but we shall assume that M = .5, so as to favor the policer over the transformer strategy as much as experience permits.

Given this specification of M, a transformer would trust her fellows only if she believed that no more than .5 of them lacked principled preferences. Thus, to develop and maintain trust, transformers must insure that no more than .5 of their number could survive without principled preferences. Over time, however, the operation of a transformer enforcement mechanism would drive the number of untransformed agents within a transformer community down to $.25N$ and keep it there. This, conjoined with our assumptions about trust, implies that transformers could nurture trust by maintaining a transformer enforcement mechanism.

We claim that transformers could nurture trust by punishing at least .38 of the violations occurring among them each round. But policers punish .43 of the violations committed during a representative round in precisely the same manner as transformers. It would seem, then, that a policer enforcement mechanism would do as well as a transformer enforcement mechanism at nurturing trust. And if policers would trust one another, we are denied a crucial premise in our argument that contractors would choose the transformer over the policer strategy.

Even if a policer enforcement mechanism had all of the qualities enabling a transformer enforcement mechanism to nurture trust, it would not necessarily do the same. Transformers enjoy trust because most of them develop an intrinsic preference for acting justly rather than unjustly. They develop such a preference through a course of conscious habituation. Were policers to engage in similar habituation, as well as empowering an enforcement mechanism, they would develop trust as well. Policers who did so, however, would not be distinct from transformers. And the claim that such agents would develop trust is no objection to our argument that contractors would choose the transformer over the policer strategy.

We have argued that contractors could induce one another to transform, and nurture trust by maintaining a responsive enforcement mechanism. One might worry, however, that the opacity of contractors would prevent an enforcement mechanism from identifying those lacking principled preferences. And unable to identify such individuals, an enforcement mechanism could not respond to increases in their numbers. But given information about the relative frequencies with which just and unjust contractors would violate rules of justice, an enforcement mechanism could extrapolate the value of k from information about the number of violations occurring each round. And contractors could obtain this information, although not costlessly. Thus, the opacity of contractors alone would not prevent them from maintaining a responsive enforcement mechanism.

Even if one accepts that contractors could maintain a responsive enforcement mechanism, one might worry that by assuming that they would do so, we differentiate their circumstances overly from our own. In our community, law enforcement clears around .45 of the violent crimes committed each year: murder, aggravated assault, rape, and robbery.[29] It clears a much smaller proportion of the property crimes committed yearly in our community: burglary, theft, and motor vehicle theft. Given the average losses involved in such property crimes, however, one would have to steal from an individual several times to inflict upon her the sort of loss associated with exploitation among our contractors. And the probability that a member of our community committing several such property crimes during a year would be caught doing so exceeds .45.[30]

A transformer enforcement mechanism, as we have characterized it, would punish $.38 + .62k$ of the violations committed each round. During a representative round, when $0 \leq k \leq .25$, a transformer enforcement mechanism would punish between .38 and .54 of the violations committed within its jurisdiction, around the proportion punished by our own enforcement mechanism.

Were k to exceed .25 by a significant amount during any round, a transformer enforcement mechanism would punish significantly more than .54 of the violations occurring that round. But we, like transformers, respond to surges in crime by intensifying our efforts to punish the criminals responsible: creating task forces, adding personnel, dedicating funds, and so on. And when crime rates dip again, we relax our enforcement efforts accordingly. Thus, that transformers operate under an enforcement mechanism which might sometimes punish more than .54 of the violations occurring among them does not differentiate their circumstances significantly from our own.

A responsive enforcement mechanism could do everything transformers require of it: alleviate the *PD* involved in acting justly rather than unjustly, induce contractors to transform themselves, and nurture trust among them. Such an enforcement mechanism might not provide transformers with the only, or even the most cost-effective, means of accomplishing these tasks. We shall, nonetheless, assume that transformers employ the responsive enforcement mechanism we have described to get them done. If there are more cost-effective means of doing so, then appealing to one of these rather than to this enforcement mechanism would only strengthen our argument for the collective rationality of self-transformation.

The Values of **b, eb, fb, gb, xb, yb,** *and* **sb.**   The term b represents the total output produced by distrustful contractors during any given round, the base cooperative output of both policers and transformers. Rather than specifying a value for b, we shall treat it as a constant, defining the other benefits and costs associated with the policer and transformer strategies in terms of it.

Both policers and transformers maintain an enforcement mechanism which punishes a proportion of the violations committed each round by permanent exclusion from cooperation. The value of cb indicates how much of their base cooperative output both spend each round to maintain such an enforcement mechanism. Since both policers and transformers pay cb, we can assign cb any value we wish without favoring either over the other. We shall suppose, somewhat arbitrarily, that $cb = .1b$, so that $c = .1$.

Transformers, unlike policers, maintain a responsive enforcement mechanism. And there are costs involved in monitoring the population of untransformed contractors within a community, and in responding to increases or decreases in this population by increasing or decreasing enforcement effectiveness. Together, these constitute the costs of responsiveness, which transformers pay over and above cb each round to maintain their enforcement mechanism. The value of db indicates their magnitude.

We shall assume that $db = .1b$. After all, to monitor the population of untransformed contractors within their community, transformers need only centralize and process information about violations acquired in the course of punishing these violations in the first place. And transformers could increase or decrease enforcement effectiveness by expanding or contracting existing enforcement programs. These observations suggest that the per round costs of responsiveness would not be as high again as cb. Nonetheless, we shall assume that $db = cb$, for by so doing, we favor the policer over the transformer strategy.

During a representative round, $1-p$ ranges between .38 and .54. In specifying the value of eb during a representative round, we shall assume that $1-p = .54$ during such a round, for the higher the value of $1-p$, the more the policer strategy pays relative to the transformer strategy. Under this assumption, transformers maintain a more effective enforcement mechanism than policers during a representative round, punishing .54 rather than .43 of the violations committed among them. Doing so would cost transformers something over and above both cb and db each round. The value of eb during a representative round indicates the magnitude of these costs during such a round.

Among contractors resembling us, the increase in costs associated with punishing .54 rather than .43 of the violations committed during a round would not be nearly so large as the increase in costs associated with punishing .43 of these violations rather than none of them. For within our community, enforcement costs can be graphed onto an s-shaped curve. It requires a large investment to maintain an enforcement mechanism capable of detecting, apprehending, processing, and penalizing even a minimal number of violators. Having made this investment, however, we can purchase gains in effectiveness for a small fraction of the resources required to attain minimal effectiveness. The cost of such gains increases more steeply only as an enforcement mechanism approaches perfect effectiveness. Since an enforcement mechanism punishing .43 of the violations committed during a round is nowhere near being perfectly effective, contractors could go from punishing .43 to punishing .54 of the violations committed during a round for a small fraction of cb. So as to favor the policer over the transformer strategy, we shall set the value of eb during a representative round as high as we can without making it a large fraction of cb. We suppose, accordingly, that $eb = .5cb$ during a representative round, so that $e = .05$ during such a round.

Perhaps we may assign an arbitrary value to cb, because both policers and transformers must pay it. But only transformers pay db and eb, and by deriving the values of *db* and *eb* from the value of *cb*, we insure that these values are equally arbitrary. And one might worry about the generality of an argument for the collective rationality of self-transformation which assumes that *db* and *eb* take particular, but arbitrarily specified, values.

But while the particular values of *db* and *eb* are arbitrary, we have argued for the appropriateness of letting $db = cb$ and $eb = .5cb$ during a representative round. And in comparing the payoffs of the policer and transformer strategies, it is the proportional relationships between *cb*, *db*, and *eb* during a representative round that matter, not the particular values associated with *db* and *eb* during such a round. We could substitute any linear transformation of the values we have assigned to *cb*, *db*, and *eb* during a representative round into the payoffs of the policer and transformer strategies without altering the relative magnitude of these payoffs. Thus, that the particular values of *db* and *eb* during a representative round are arbitrary does nothing to compromise the generality of our argument for the collective rationality of self-transformation.

The terms *xb* and *yb* represent the proportion of their base cooperative output that punishing any given violation costs policers and transformers *in toto*, respectively. To calculate *xb* and *yb*, we must determine 1) how much of their cooperative output policers and transformers would forfeit punishing any given violation, and 2) how much policers and transformers would spend punishing any given violation.

As *xb* and *yb* increase, so does the payoff of the transformer strategy relative to that of the policer strategy. Because we seek to favor the latter over the former, we shall specify *xb* and *yb* conservatively.

By excluding a violator from cooperation during a round, both policers and transformers would forfeit $1/N$ of their base cooperative output for that round. Given our specification of *N*, this amounts to .00001*b*. Transformers would incur an additional loss in excluding a violator from cooperation during a round, forfeiting $1/N$ of the increase they realize from trust during that round. Given our specification of *N*, this amounts to .00001*sb*, or .000001*b*. We shall assume that contractors would spend as much each round punishing any given violation as the responsible party would have contributed to their base cooperative output that round were she not being punished. This amounts to .00001*b* among policers and .000011*b* among transformers. Given this assumption, it would cost policers .00002*b* per round, and transformers .000022*b* per round, to punish any given violation.

If contractors summarily executed or banished violators, then *xb* and *yb* would reduce to the per round cost of punishing policers and transformers, respectively. In our own community, of course, we do not summarily execute or banish violators. And because we do not do so, the costs of punishing any given violation virtually always extend over many years.

In the interests of specifying xb and yb conservatively, however, we shall assume that for both policers and transformers, the cost of punishing any given violation reduces to the per round cost of punishing that violation. And given this assumption, $xb = .00002b$ and $yb = .000022b$, so that $x = .00002$ and $y = .000022$.[31]

Given the values of w and $1-p$ during a representative round, transformers would punish between $.021N$ and $.03N$ violations during such a round. And given the values of v and $1-o$ during a representative round, policers would punish $.054N$ violations during such a round. But punishing at least 180% of the violations transformers punish during a representative round, one might expect that punishing any given violation would cost policers less than it would transformers during such a round. Appealing to an economics of scale, one might object that our specification of xb and yb illicitly advantages transformers over policers, at least during a representative round.

But punishing any given violation does cost policers less than it costs transformers during a representative round, $.00002b$ instead of $.000022b$. Thus, on our account, policers do benefit from an economics of scale.

And there is reason to think our charging transformers $.1$ more than policers to punish any given violation during a representative round is sufficiently generous to the faker strategy. For transformers maintain an enforcement infrastructure at least as large as the one maintained by policers during any given round, paying at least as much to maintain it as policers do. They maintain such an infrastructure, however many violations they are punishing during a round, so as to retain the capacity to respond to increases in k by punishing between $.38$ and 1 of the violations committed during a round on very short notice. Because maintaining an enforcement infrastructure is by far the largest part of the cost of punishing any given violation, at least among contractors resembling us, transformers would never have to pay much more than policers to punish any given violation of rules of justice.

Finally, we shall specify sb, which represents the increase in their base cooperative output transformers realize each round by transforming themselves. In specifying sb, we shall assume that contractors would have the same number of cooperative opportunities whether they were to become policers or transformers.[32] And we shall assume that contractors can be exploited no more than once each round.[33]

Contractors can get away with exploiting one another under any imperfectly effective enforcement mechanism. And interacting in different situations, an imperfectly effective enforcement mechanism would protect contractors differentially. By analyzing the different sorts of situations in which they interact, contractors can distinguish more and less risky cooperative opportunities.

Given our specification of v, policers can expect approximately .125 of their number to be exploited during a representative round. By identifying the riskiest .125 cooperative opportunities within her community during any such round, and by declining any such opportunities to which she might be exposed in the course of interacting with her partner, a policer protects herself from both exploitation and punishment without diminishing her expectations. We shall assume that, concerned to satisfy her preferences as fully as possible, each would decline what she sees as the riskiest .125 cooperative opportunities within her community during a representative round should she be exposed to any of these in the course of interacting with her partner.

Given our specification of w during a representative round, transformers can expect approximately .055 of their number to be exploited during any such round. But having transformed themselves, and developed trust, transformers would cooperate even where their enforcement mechanism would provide them with little or no protection from exploitation.[34] Hence, transformers would capitalize on all of the risky cooperative opportunities during a representative round that policers would decline.

Given our assumption that policers and transformers would have the same number of cooperative opportunities, this implies that transformers would engage in at least .125 more cooperative interactions than policers during a representative round. Because individual policers might have different ideas about the riskiest .125 cooperative opportunities among them during such a round, transformers might cooperate even more relative to policers than we have described. We shall assume, however, that transformers would engage in precisely .125 more cooperative interactions than policers during a representative round, for doing so favors the policer over the transformer strategy. And we shall suppose that engaging in .125 more cooperative interactions during a representative round than they would were they policers, transformers would realize a .125 gain in their base cooperative output, so that during such a round, $sb = .125b$ and $s = .125$.

The Solution to this Decision Problem

Since contractors' decision problem involves neither strategic interaction nor uncertainty, solving it is a simple exercise in decision theory. For our contractors to choose the transformer over the policer strategy in this problem, the expected payoff of the former must be greater than that of the latter. That is, it must be the case that

$$(b+sb) - [(cb + db + eb) + (1-p)(w/100)Nyb] >$$
$$b - (cb + (1-o)(v/100)Nxb).$$

Simplifying this inequality yields the requirement that

$$s + N[(v/100)(1{-}o)x - (w/100)(1{-}p)y] > d + e.$$

Substituting the values of d, e, N, $1{-}o$, $1{-}p$, s, v, w, x, and y during a representative round (collected in Table 4.1) into this inequality yields the following expression:

$$.125 + (100,000)[(.125)(.43)(.00002) - (.055)(.54)(.000022)] > .1 + .05.$$

If we do the requisite arithmetic, we find that this reduces to the claim that $.167 > .15$. Since this claim is true, the transformer strategy promises our contractors a higher payoff than the policer strategy in their decision problem. Thus, our contractors would jointly choose the transformer over the policer strategy in their decision problem. And thus, at the first stage of their choice situation, our contractors would choose a joint strategy requiring them to transform themselves.

One might worry about the robustness of this result, for it appears to require that c, d, N, $1{-}o$, $1{-}p$, s, v, w, x, and y take just the values during a representative round that we have specified, while we might plausibly have assigned different values to these terms. I have several replies to this worry.

First, these terms need not take just the values we have specified for contractors to jointly choose the transformer over the policer strategy. We can perturb all of these values slightly, and some of them considerably, without altering the solution to the decision problem involved in implementing rules of justice.

Second, and more importantly, we have not assigned random values to these terms. Rather, in specifying these terms, we have sought to suggest conditions within our own community, as our project requires. And we have favored the policer over the transformer strategy as much as this requirement permits. Hence, if we have erred in specifying the payoffs of contractors' decision problem, we have erred by favoring the policer over

Table 4.1   The Values of d, e, N, o, p, s, v, w, x, and y during a Representative Round

$d = .1$	$s = .125$
$e = .05$	$v = 12.5$
$N = 100,000$	$w = 5.5$
$o = .57$	$x = .000022$
$p = .46$	$y = .00002$

the transformer strategy more than we should have. Any corrections to these payoffs would only bolster our account of its solution.

Third, and finally, that this decision problem would involve a different solution were we to perturb its payoffs sufficiently in no way compromises our project. Self-transformation is a rational joint strategy under some conditions only. Under other conditions, the policer strategy may be a rational joint strategy. For our purposes, it suffices that the payoffs of contractors' decision problem suggest the conditions under which we live. Versions of it involving other payoffs have little interest for us.

Implementing the Transformer Strategy

Having jointly chosen the transformer over the policer strategy, contractors could advance to the second stage of their choice situation only by taking whatever measures are required to insure that they can execute this strategy successfully. Our treatment of possible solutions to the *PD* involved in complying with rules of justice implies that to execute the transformer strategy successfully, contractors must empower an enforcement mechanism. But while contractors choosing the transformer strategy would all benefit by empowering a transformer enforcement mechanism and advancing to the second stage of their choice situation, each would benefit even more were this to occur without her having contributed anything to transformer enforcement. Worse, were too many contractors to seek the latter benefit, all contributions to transformer enforcement would be in vain. Appealing to the free-rider and assurance problems involved in empowering a transformer enforcement mechanism, one might argue that our contractors could not empower such an enforcement mechanism. And appealing to the unfortunate consequences of remaining mired at the first stage of their choice situation, one might argue that our contractors would reject any joint strategy at this stage which could not but leave them so mired.[35]

But our contractors could empower a transformer enforcement mechanism. To establish this, we divide doing so into two problems, the provider-selection problem and the empowerment problem, and argue that contractors could resolve both of these.[36]

In so arguing, we shall assume again that contractors follow one of the decision rules among which the decision value framework arbitrates, the expected utility principle. By so doing, we simplify our analysis of the provider-selection and empowerment problems. And besides, facing these problems, contractors would choose in the same manner were they maximizing expected utility or maximizing decision value.[37]

The Provider-Selection Problem

Empowering a transformer enforcement mechanism, contractors must first select one of their number to direct their enforcement efforts.[38] Call the problem involved in doing so the *provider-selection problem.*

The provider-selection problem has both of the characteristic features of a coordination problem. First, it has multiple *coordination equilibria,* combinations of strategies in which no agent would be better off if any single agent chose differently.[39] Indeed, there are as many coordination equilibria in this problem as there are potential enforcement providers. And second, although there is a significant conflict of interest in this problem, coordination of interest predominates. Each contractor prefers realizing one of the available coordination equilibria, even if it is not the one she most prefers, to a failure to coordinate. If we think of games in terms of a range, with games of pure coordination at one end and games of pure conflict at the other, the provider-selection problem falls nearer to the former end than to the latter.[40]

To resolve such an impure coordination problem, one need only bring rational agents to believe that one of its coordination equilibria is *salient,* that it stands out from the rest in a unique and conspicuous manner. Given this belief, each would expect others to do their parts in bringing about this outcome. And in the face of such expectations, expected utility reasoning would tell each to do her part in bringing about this outcome, even when it is not the one she prefers most.[41]

Margaret Gilbert argues that in the absence of information grounding a background belief that others would do their part in bringing about a salient equilibrium, salience provides rational agents with no reasons for choosing such an equilibrium. She concludes that salience is not intrinsically action-guiding, at least not for rational agents pared down to their essential features.[42]

We need not refute Gilbert to show that our contractors could solve the provider-selection problem. For our contractors are not rational agents pared down to their essential features. Rather, they have fully-developed personal and social characteristics, and access to all the information the natural and social sciences supply to us. And evidence from the social sciences suggests that when we find ourselves in coordination problems, we pursue a salient equilibrium, if there is one, with a much higher frequency than we pursue other equilibria.[43] Thus, contractors have reason to believe that their fellows would do their part in bringing about a salient equilibrium within the provider-selection problem, if it turns out to have one.

Initially, none of the coordination equilibria of the provider-selection problem are salient. But contractors have available a device for making one of these equilibria salient. They could select an enforcement-provider by means of an election.

On the first ballot, each would no doubt vote for herself, yielding a stalemate. But knowing that they must resolve this stalemate to advance to the second stage of their choice situation, each would have some reason to back someone besides herself on the second ballot. And some contractors would have more reason to do so than others. Some, given their preferences, would rank being enforcement-provider higher than others. Some, given their advantageous social characteristics, would have less to lose than others by holding out to become enforcement-provider. And some, as the result of personal characteristics rendering them averse to risk, would be less inclined than others to risk permanent stalemate by so holding out. As the result of such factors, at least some contractors would have sufficient reason to vote for someone besides themselves on the second ballot. Voting rationally on the second ballot, such contractors would break the stalemate yielded by the first.

On subsequent ballots, some would emerge as front-runners, with those receiving the fewest votes dropping out because they could expect to get no more votes on future ballots from an electorate concerned to settle upon an enforcement-provider. Eventually, the ballot would be winnowed to two candidates. And the one receiving the most votes on this ballot would be the uniquely conspicuous, and thus salient, choice as enforcement-provider. Given the argument developed above for the rationality of contributing to a salient coordination equilibrium, contractors would agree that this individual should direct their enforcement efforts, resolving the enforcement-provider problem.

One might worry, however, that the losers of this election would simply refuse to accept its results, demanding a new election. And one might worry that given such a precedent, the losers of any successive election would do the same, yielding an enduring stalemate at the first stage of contractors' choice situation. Appealing to this worry, one might object that contractors could not resolve the enforcement-provider problem by means of an election.

Resembling the members of our community, most of our contractors are uncharismatic, lacking the qualities which would make them contenders in a subsequent election. Lacking such qualities, they have nothing to gain by holding out for a new election. And they have a lot to lose by so doing. For in successfully holding out for a new election, they would set a precedent encouraging others to reject the results of all subsequent elections, leaving contractors in a permanent stalemate at the first stage of their choice situation. Conversely, by accepting the results of their first election, uncharismatic contractors lose nothing at all. For lacking the qualities which would make them contenders in a subsequent election, they lose nothing if such an election is never held.

With nothing to gain, and much to lose, by holding out for a new election, all uncharismatic contractors would accept the results of their first election.

And this renders it rational for all charismatic contractors to accept these results as well. For it would be rational for a charismatic contractor to hold out for a new election only if by doing so, she could hope to render salient the coordination equilibrium in which she serves as enforcement-provider. But with over half of her fellows unwilling to have a new election, much less to vote for her, holding out for a new election could not accomplish this result. Preferring coordination on some equilibrium to a failure to coordinate, and with her most preferred equilibrium unavailable, it would be rational for every charismatic contractor to accept the coordination equilibrium picked out by contractors' first election.

Duncan MacIntosh has a more general worry about the proposal that rational agents could resolve coordination problems by means of equilibrium-selecting devices.[44] Given a choice between several such devices among which they are indifferent, rational agents must coordinate on one such device before they can use it to resolve any coordination problem. But if they were indifferent between several equilibrium-selecting devices, rationality alone would not provide agents with a means of picking out one such device as authoritative. Thus, concludes MacIntosh, in the absence of certain happy contingencies, ideally rational agents could not resolve coordination problems in which the only obstacle to coordination is an absence of agreement on an equilibrium-selecting device.

This conclusion would appear to undermine our account of how rational contractors could resolve the enforcement-provider problem. But we do not have to refute MacIntosh's argument to show that our contractors could resolve the enforcement-provider problem as we have described. For our contractors occupy a choice situation characterized by contingencies enabling them to coordinate on an equilibrium-selecting device. Having differing personal characteristics, they would be differentially obstinate, and differentially risk-averse. And as the result of their differing preferences and social characteristics, they would have different stakes in resolving the enforcement-provider problem. Did our contractors not agree upon the same equilibrium-selecting device initially, it would be rational for the less well-situated to adopt the equilibrium-selecting device proposed by the best-situated.[45] Thus, because of the contingencies characterizing their choice situation, our contractors could coordinate upon voting as a means for resolving the enforcement-provider problem.

The Empowerment Problem

The enforcement-provider could provide contractors with a transformer enforcement mechanism only if enough of them would obey her commands. Call the problem involved in bringing contractors to do so the *empowerment problem*.

The enforcement-provider could induce contractors to obey her commands by offering them sufficiently large positive incentives to do so. And since contractors would agree to empower a transformer enforcement mechanism, the enforcement-provider would have access to the resources required to fund such incentives, at least in theory. But rationality requires each of our contractors to free-ride on her fellows' enforcement contributions if she can get away with doing so. Thus, if she is to induce contractors to obey her commands by offering them positive incentives, the enforcement-provider requires some means of assembling the resources required to fund such incentives from her recalcitrant fellows.

She could do so by dispatching small cadres of contractors to collect these funds. All share an interest in having such cadres formed, for each does better with a transformer enforcement mechanism than without one. But there is an element of conflict involved in the formation of such cadres as well. Since cadre membership would involve time and effort, at best, and risk to life and limb, at worst, each contractor would prefer not serving on such a cadre to serving on it. The formation of collection cadres, thus, constitutes an impure coordination problem.

By appointing contractors to cadres in such a way that serving would cost each less than functioning without a transformer enforcement mechanism, the enforcement-provider could insure that contractors' interest in coordinating predominates within this problem. And by appointing just enough contractors to each cadre to make it effective in collecting from its targets, the enforcement-provider could mark off one of the equilibria of this problem as salient. From our previous argument that rational parties to an impure coordination problem involving more convergence than conflict of interests would each do her part in bringing about a salient equilibrium, we can conclude that contractors would serve on the collection cadres to which they were appointed.

By deploying enough small collection cadres, the enforcement-provider could amass the resources required to induce contractors to serve on a permanent enforcement cadre, and to train them to do so. Once sufficient contractors have been enlisted and trained to do what is required to implement the transformer strategy, the resulting enforcement cadre could take over the task of assembling the resources required for its own maintenance. And once a self-sustaining cadre of contractors led by positive incentives to perform the tasks required to implement the transformer strategy is in place, the enforcement-provider has solved the empowerment problem.

One might worry that each contractor appointed to a collection cadre would refuse to serve out of fear that others appointed to that cadre would refuse to serve, rendering her own service vain. And were this the case, the enforcement-provider could not assemble enough resources to empower a transformer enforcement mechanism. But contractors do not risk such an uncompensated expenditure in joining a small collection cadre, for each can confirm for herself whether all those appointed to her cadre join it. And each can monitor the performance of her fellows in the course of her cadre's functioning, so as to determine whether each is serving as appointed. Thus, because of the nature of service on a small collection cadre, contractors need not worry about being caught out by the desertion of other cadre members.[46]

Or one might worry that contractors appointed to a collection cadre would refuse to serve out of the fear that those appointed to *other* cadres would refuse to serve, so that despite their best efforts, insufficient resources would be assembled to empower a transformer enforcement mechanism. But the enforcement-provider could resolve this problem simply by allowing the members of each small cadre to divide up their take as compensation for time and effort expended if all of the cadres together fail to assemble enough resources to empower a transformer enforcement mechanism.

Or one might worry that collection cadres would themselves abscond with whatever resources they had managed to assemble before a transformer enforcement mechanism could even be empowered. But to prevent this, an enforcement-provider need only send each cadre after few enough resources that its members would gain less by splitting their take than each would lose were a transformer enforcement mechanism not empowered as the result of their absconding with their assigned take. And she could prevent cadres from collecting more than their assigned take by appointing to each a combination of contractors capable of effectively transporting and protecting no more than its assigned take.

One last concern: one might worry that members of a permanent enforcement cadre, being concerned to satisfy their own preferences, would be little concerned with enforcing rules of justice. The enforcement-provider can hardly be trusted to keep her underlings in line, for she too is concerned to satisfy her own preferences. There is, thus, a possibility that those serving within a transformer enforcement mechanism would neglect their enforcement tasks, using their position solely to enrich themselves.

Contractors could foreclose this possibility by structuring their enforcement mechanism appropriately. To keep their enforcement-provider interested in performing her charged task, contractors need only limit the term of her office, and arrange for periodic elections to fill it. In such a context, the enforcement-provider would be motivated to perform her charged task by the desire to retain the benefits associated with her office.[47]

And there are techniques by means of which an enforcement-provider who was so motivated could keep her underlings in line. By dividing enforcement tasks among contractors, and by dividing the resources required to perform these tasks similarly, the enforcement-provider could make it difficult for her underlings to overstep the authority granted them. And by setting her underlings the task of policing one another, and providing them incentives to do so, the enforcement-provider could dissuade them from misusing the authority granted them. By an appropriate combination of such techniques, the enforcement-provider could bring most of the members of a permanent enforcement cadre to perform the tasks assigned them, yielding a functional transformer enforcement mechanism.

Conclusion

In this chapter, we have argued that at the first stage of their choice situation, contractors would choose a joint strategy requiring most of them to transform themselves. From this, it follows that self-transformation is collectively rational for them.

Given the structure of their choice situation, contractors can hope to satisfy their preferences only by advancing to its second stage. And, given the assumptions of our analysis, contractors choosing the transformer strategy can do so only by empowering a transformer enforcement mechanism. From this, our argument that contractors would choose the transformer strategy, and our argument that they could empower a transformer enforcement mechanism, we can conclude that upon choosing the transformer strategy, they would empower a transformer enforcement mechanism, advancing to the second stage of their choice situation. We consider what contractors would choose at this stage in the next several chapters.

Notes

1. We shall argue that contractors would be choosing between two joint strategies for implementing rules of justice. Both of these involve the same worst outcome, contractors failing to implement rules of justice. Thus, maximin fails to distinguish between them. And of these two strategies, the one maximizing expected utility for contractors also offers them the highest probability of implementing rules of justice successfully and thus avoiding a disastrous outcome altogether. Thus, expected utility and disaster avoidance reasoning converge in their recom-

mendations to contractors about what joint strategy to choose. And thus, the joint strategy maximizing expected utility for contractors also maximizes decision value for them.

2. We assume that rounds of interaction last for a year for two reasons: 1) to make plausible our later assumption that losing all of the resources she has invested in an interaction is disastrous for a contractor, and 2) to facilitate comparisons between our choice situation and our own community, in which major social and economic indicators are usually expressed *per annum*.

3. Let letters represent possible outcomes a contractor might choose in any interaction. In particular, let *C* = comply with rules of justice and *D* = violate rules of justice. Let pairs of letters (*DC, CC,* and so on) represent the possible outcomes of interactions. And finally, let orderings of such pairs from left to right represent an ordering of the possible outcomes of any such interaction from most to least preferred.

4. In so analyzing the PD, I am following David Schmidtz. See David Schmidtz, *The Limits of Government* (Boulder: Westview Press, 1991), 57–61.

5. This account of the assurance problem is Schmidtz's. See Schmidtz, 60. For the standard account, see Amartya Sen, "Isolation, Assurance, and the Social Rate of Discount," *Quarterly Journal of Economics* 81 (1967): 112–24.

6. Action *A* dominates action *B* for player *P* just in case choosing *A* would yield *P* a higher-ranked outcome than choosing *B* no matter what actions her fellows were to choose.

7. This classification of cooperative solutions to the PD is MacIntosh's. See Duncan MacIntosh, "McClennen's Early Co-operative Solution To The Prisoner's Dilemma," *The Southern Journal of Philosophy* 29 (1991): 341–58.

8. See Lawrence Davis, "Prisoners, Paradox, and Rationality," in *Paradoxes of Rationality and Cooperation,* ed. Richmond Campbell and Lanning Sowden (Vancouver: University of British Columbia Press, 1985), 45–59.

9. One can read David Gauthier as offering an alternative principle solution to the PD. For a revised theory of instrumental rationality supporting such a solution to the PD, see David Gauthier, "In the Neighborhood of the Newcomb-Predictor," *Proceedings of the Aristotelian Society* 89 (1988–89): 179–94.

10. The most prominent example of a resolution solution to the PD is E. F. McClennen's account of resolute choice. For a discussion of this account, see the previous chapter.

11. I learned this line of argument from Duncan MacIntosh. For a more detailed presentation of it, and a discussion of various objections to it, See Duncan MacIntosh, "Libertarian Agency and Rational Morality: Action-Theoretic Objections To Gauthier's Dispositional Solution of the Compliance Problem," *The Southern Journal of Philosophy* 26 (1988): 499–525.

12. For a discussion of assurance contracts, see Schmidtz, 66–96.

13. Classically, public goods are defined by jointness of supply (one person's consumption of a good does not reduce the amount available to anyone else), and nonexcludability (it is impossible to prevent those not contributing to a good from consuming it). See Mancur Olson, Jr., *The Logic of Collective Action* (Cambridge: Harvard University Press, 1965), 14–6.

14. One might think that such assurance contracts would not work in the absence of the state. David Schmidtz argues that this is not so. See Schmidtz, 66–96.

15. After all, widespread possession of such a disposition in a community exhibits jointness of supply, and to a great degree, nonexcludability.

16. I once saw an episode of *Star Trek,* for instance, in which the members of one community were monitored, judged, and punished by means of thought-detecting, pain-dealing necklets controlled by a central computer. And in George Orwell's *1984,* a enforcement mechanism like ours is supplemented by two-way televisions, an elaborate network of secret informants, and an effective force of secret police. See George Orwell, *1984* (New York: Harcourt, Brace, and Co., 1949).

17. A caning might satisfy the preferences of a graffiti artist intent on abasing herself. Imprisonment might be regarded as a blessing by someone with agoraphobia. And even the death penalty would not count as a punishment if inflicted upon a violator who wants to die, but cannot bear to kill herself.

18. Contractors might accomplish such exclusion in various ways, by blacklisting, banishing, imprisoning, fining, or even executing violators. There are advantages and disadvantages associated with each of these penalties. For our purposes, it does not matter which of these penalties contractors select, so we shall not treat this matter further.

19. For simplicity's sake, we charge policers and transformers a lump sum to penalize each violator they apprehend. For all that we have said, however, contractors may employ penalties extending over many rounds. We shall assume that each time contractors employ such a penalty, they set aside the funds required to impose it on the violator in question, then pay for doing so out of these funds.

20. Policers' enforcement needs might vary from round to round as well, so that they, too, would have to pay d. Favoring the policer over the transformer strategy, however, we shall assume that policers' enforcement needs would remain constant from round to round.

21. For an argument to this effect, see the section of Chapter 7 entitled "The Iterated Sense of Justice Game."

22. See the Federal Bureau of Investigation, *Uniform Crime Reports for the United States* (Washington, D. C.: U. S. Government Printing Office, 1995), 58.

23. For a discussion of these payoffs and a defense of this assumption, see Chapter 7.

24. The term $o(2) + (1-o)(-1)$ represents the expected payoff of defecting in a policer community, while the term $(.875)(1) + (.125)(-1)$ represents the expected payoff of cooperating in such a community, given the value we have assigned to v.

25. For a defense of this specification of these values, see Chapter 7.

26. The term $p(4) + (1-p)(-2)$ represents the expected payoff of defecting in a transformer community, while the term $(.945)(2) + (.055)(-2)$ represents the expected payoff of cooperating in such a community, given the value we have assigned to w.

27. A sociological study by Eisenstadt and Roniger provides some corroboration for this account of trust as a threshold phenomenon. They claim that trust "assumes the maintenance of mutual obligations," and that institutionalizing re-

spect for basic entitlements and rights is one important means of preventing the breakdown of trust in advanced societies. See S. N. Eisenstadt and L. Roniger, *Persons, Clients, and Friends: Interpersonal Relations and the Structure of Trust in Society* (Cambridge: Cambridge University Press, 1984), 29–42.

28. We assume that individuals willing to exploit their fellows will do so periodically. Among flawed individuals living under an imperfectly effective enforcement mechanism, this is a safe assumption.

29. A crime is cleared when at least one person has been arrested for it, charged with it, and turned over to the courts for prosecution. Sometimes, we clear crimes committed one year during a subsequent year. So as to avoid needless complexity, we do not incorporate this feature of our own circumstances into contractors' decision problem.

30. All of the above claims are based on data about crime within our community over the past ten years. See the Federal Bureau of Investigation, *Uniform Crime Reports for the United States* (Washington, D. C.: U. S. Government Printing Office, 1986–95).

31. In specifying xb and yb, we have disregarded the savings that both policers and transformers would realize in punishing violations committed by the same contractor. But given how we conceive of interaction among contractors, none could benefit from violating rules of justice more than once per round, so none would so violate.

32. Among opaque contractors, this assumption is plausible.

33. This is plausible because a contractor would pose little threat to others while recovering from being exploited, and would have little left to tempt others to exploit her again.

34. What use would a community split between possessors of principled preferences and those who prey upon them have for trust? None, but given the turnover within a transformer community due to violators being punished, deaths, births, immigration, and emigration, not all transformers would possess principled preferences during any given round. Trust brings transformers in the process of developing principled preferences to capitalize on risky cooperative opportunities.

35. I thank David Estlund for suggesting this objection to me.

36. Here I adapt Jean Hampton's account of how Hobbesian people could empower a sovereign to my own purposes. See Jean Hampton, *Hobbes and the Social Contract Tradition* (Cambridge: Cambridge University Press, 1986), 147–86.

37. Empowering a transformer enforcement mechanism involves a pair of coordination problems. Maximin fails to distinguish between any of the options in either of these problems because all involve the same worst outcome, failure to coordinate. And of these options, the ones maximizing expected utility for contractors also offer them the highest problem of coordinating and thus avoiding a disastrous outcome altogether. Thus, expected utility and disaster avoidance reasoning converge in their recommendations to contractors in both of these coordination problems. And thus, what maximizes expected utility for contractors facing the provider-selection and empowerment problems also maximizes decision value for them.

38. Contractors might, of course, select a set of individuals to direct their enforcement efforts, but this does not pose a problem appreciably different than the one involved in selecting a single individual to do so.

39. For this definition of coordination equilibria, see David Lewis, *Convention: A Philosophical Study* (Cambridge: Harvard University Press, 1969), 14.

40. For the suggestion that we think of games in terms of such a range, see Thomas Schelling, *The Strategy of Conflict* (Cambridge: Harvard University Press, 1960), 83–118 and 291–303.

41. For a detailed account of what expected utility reasoning involves in strategic contexts, see Chapter 7.

42. See Margaret Gilbert, "Rationality and Salience," *Philosophical Studies* 57 (1989): 61–77.

43. See, for instance, the experimental evidence reported in Schelling, Chapter 3.

44. See Duncan MacIntosh, "Buridan and the Circumstances of Justice (On the Implications of the Rational Unsolvability of Certain Co-ordination Problems)," *Pacific Philosophical Quarterly* 73 (1992): 150–73.

45. What if two or more individuals were tied for being the best-situated, and chose different equilibrium-selecting devices? Then the one to gain the most adherents first would be better-situated, and others should accept her device. What if equal numbers of adherents flocked to each of the best-situated? Then the one with the best-situated adherents would be better-situated, and again, the others should concede. But what if equal numbers of equally well-situated adherents flocked to each of the best-situated? Such a stalemate would be tremendously unstable, for the loss of any advantage by any member of any camp would make it rational for all that camp's members to concede to someone better-situated, at which point all members of all other camps should concede to this individual as well.

46. But what if cadre members could not each monitor one another's activities constantly? In such a case, a cadre member who performs her part unilaterally risks expending time and effort without realizing any benefit from doing so, suffering a net loss. And one might worry that in such situations, no rational cadre member would do her assigned tasks. For a discussion of various means by which rational agents could resolve such free-rider problems, see Jean Hampton, "Free-Rider Problems in the Production of Collective Goods," *Economics and Philosophy* 3 (1987): 245–73.

47. Might an enforcement-provider not decide to remain in office permanently, enforcing her decision with her enforcement cadre? And freed from the burden of having to win the next election, might she not forego enforcing rules of justice in favor of using her enforcement cadre to pursue her own ends? For an argument that rational subjects retain the power to fire their rulers in some circumstances, and that this suffices to keep rulers from overstepping the limits placed by subjects on their power, see Hampton, *Hobbes and the Social Contract Tradition*, 220–34.

5

Maximin Reasoning

Let a *transformer community* be a group of agents who have jointly chosen the transformer strategy, and taken the measures required to insure that they can execute it. Having formed a transformer community at the first stage of their choice situation, contractors must choose an individual strategy for satisfying their preferences within such a community at its second stage. But that self-transformation is collectively rational for contractors does not imply that each would act rationally by transforming herself. For self-transformation imposes costs on individuals. And if its net payoff is less than the net payoff of some other individual strategy available to contractors, it would not be individually rational for them to transform themselves.

Because contractors are opaque, their choices of individual strategies would not affect the willingness of others to interact with them. Thus, contractors can expect to interact with others roughly as frequently over their cooperative lifetimes whatever individual strategy they choose. And given that this is so, we can establish the individual rationality of self-transformation by showing that were they choosing individual strategies during a representative round, contractors would choose one requiring them to transform themselves.

The Individual Strategies Available to Contractors

In order to establish this result, we must specify the individual strategies available to transformers. During each round of interaction within a transformer community, contractors have the same two moves available to them. Each might, by complying with rules of justice, cooperate in the prisoner's dilemma (*PD*) involved in acting justly rather than unjustly. Alternatively, each might, by violating these rules, defect in this *PD*.[1]

Cooperation in this *PD*, as we shall conceive of it, involves each member of an interacting pair investing resources in some joint project, with each recouping her original investment along with a share of its return. Defection in this *PD*, as we shall conceive of it, involves one or both of them both members of a pair investing resources in a joint project, then trying to seize all that has been invested in this project, and its entire return, for herself.

At the second stage of their choice situation, contractors do not choose between cooperation and defection directly. Rather, they choose among strategies governing their behavior during future rounds of interaction within a transformer community. As we shall conceive of these, they are dispositions controlling the frequency with which contractors cooperate and defect during future rounds.

Faced with such a choice, a contractor might choose to transform herself. Having developed principled preferences, she would value possible outcomes in which she acts justly more than any other possible outcomes of her actions. And she would act unjustly only by mistake, as infrequently as she could given her flaws. Call this the *true transformer* strategy.

Alternatively, a contractor might pretend to transform herself without really doing so.[2] Such a contractor would value acting justly rather than unjustly for purely instrumental reasons. She would defect on her partner whenever doing so would best serve her preferences, acting unjustly as frequently as she could given her rationality. Call this the *faker* strategy.

The faker and true transformer strategies are the endpoints of a range of individual strategies available to transformers, each involving a different probability mixture over cooperation and defection. But determining the payoff to contractors of every strategy on this range would be a daunting task, so we shall restrict their options to the two we have defined.

These two strategies have special significance for us. The true transformer strategy models possession of the sense of justice. And the faker strategy models the lack of such a disposition. Since we are engaged in showing that contractors would do better to develop the sense of justice than to refrain from doing so, our focus on the faker and true transformer strategies is appropriate.

If contractors would do better choosing some strategy on the range between the faker and true transformer strategies than they would choosing either of these strategies, then so restricting their options would compromise our justification of the sense of justice. But we shall argue that most would do better to cooperate than to defect during a representative round, so that most maximize decision value by choosing the true transformer over the faker strategy. If successful, this argument establishes that most maximize decision value by choosing the true transformer strategy over anything else on the range between the faker and true transformer strategies. For each strategy on this range requires contractors to cooperate less frequently and defect more frequently than true trans-formers. Thus, our argument that most contractors would choose the true transformer over the faker strategy can be generalized to show that most would choose the true transformer strategy over anything on the range between these two strategies. And thus, we do not compromise our justi-fication of the sense of justice by restricting contractors' options to the faker and true transformer strategies.

Some More Assumptions of Our Analysis

In applying maximin, disaster avoidance, and expected utility reasoning to the choice between the faker and true transformer strategies, we in-voke a number of assumptions, both substantive and simplifying. Here we explicate and motivate these assumptions.

First, we shall assume that transformers are making a one-time choice between the faker and true transformer strategies, choosing a disposition once and for all to govern their behavior in future interactions.[3]

This assumption is especially plausible in the case of transformers choosing the true transformer strategy. Having developed principled preferences, a contractor most prefers to cooperate when interacting with others, whether these others cooperate or defect. And within a trans-former community, the true transformer strategy promises flawed con-tractors better odds of realizing an outcome in which she cooperates than the policer strategy. Thus, it is plausible to think that transformers choos-ing the true transformer strategy make a one-time choice because they would never have an incentive to change strategies. Quite the contrary, such contractors would maximize by reaffirming the true transformer strategy.

A transformer choosing the faker strategy would have incentive to change strategies, and opportunity to do so, but not typically at the same time. A successful faker, one who has not been punished for acting un-justly, would have opportunity to change strategies. But given the moti-vational inertia which characterizes shallowly rational agents, doing so would cost her time and effort. And enjoying a higher payoff than she would as a true transformer, such an agent would typically have no in-centive to become a true transformer even if doing so would cost her nothing at all. Failed fakers, being punished by a transformer enforce-ment mechanism, would have neither incentive nor opportunity to switch strategies.

There are possible conditions under which it would be rational for suc-cessful fakers to pay the costs involved in switching strategies. A faker's gifts, for instance, might decay so much that she could expect to do bet-ter by switching to the true transformer strategy than by remaining a faker. But building this possibility into our account would set up a one-way flow of contractors from the faker to the true transformer strategy, reducing each true transformer's odds of being exploited by a faker during any given interaction. Favoring the faker over the true transformer strategy, we shall disregard this possibility.

Second, we assume that contractors have available a common medium of exchange, like money, and that the resources each has available for pursuing her preferences can be measured in terms of this medium. By means of this assumption, we simplify the task of comparing contractors' resource endowments on each of the possible outcomes of their choice between the faker and true transformer strategies, and we represent accurately our own circumstances.

Third, we assume that utility payoffs vary in a constant and linear fashion with resource endowments. The relationship between resources and utility is almost certainly messier than this among us. But by means of this assumption, we simplify the task of specifying utility payoffs to contractors on the possible outcomes of their choice between the faker and the true transformer strategies. And, as we shall argue in specifying these payoffs, we do so in a way which favors the faker over the true transformer strategy. That contractors have this information about the relationship between resources and utility available follows from our assumption that they have access to the sorts of techniques, data, information, and predictions supplied us by the natural and social sciences.

Fourth, in calculating contractors' payoffs on the true transformer strategy, we shall disregard the utility each would realize from satisfying her intrinsic preference for acting justly rather than unjustly, for two reasons. First, when they choose strategies, our contractors do not yet possess an intrinsic preference for acting justly rather than unjustly. And given our assumption of present-aim rationality, the satisfaction of a preference contractors do not possess when they choose strategies cannot affect the payoffs associated with the possible outcomes of this choice. Second, and more importantly, no justification of the sense of justice appealing to the utility true transformers would realize from acting justly rather than unjustly would be fundamental. Hence, to succeed at our project, we must disregard the utility generated by the satisfaction of principled preferences in arguing for the rationality of choosing the true transformer over the faker strategy. And besides, admitting such utility into our argument for the rationality of choosing the faker over the true transformer strategy would only reinforce its conclusion.

Fifth, we assume that contractors always invest the same proportion of their available resources in interaction, and that each always seeks out a partner with as much to invest in interaction as she. By means of this assumption, we simplify the task of assigning payoffs to contractors for co-operation and defection without favoring either of their available strategies over the other.

Sixth, we assume that each contractor invests a large proportion of her available resources in every interaction in which she participates, enough so that their loss would constitute a disaster for her whatever her social characteristics. Were it rational for contractors to maintain principled preferences when they risk so much by doing so, maintaining principled preferences under less risky conditions would be no less rational for them.

Seventh, we assume that in cooperating, a contractor devotes to some joint project all the resources she invests in interaction. We assume also that when both members of a pair cooperate, each recoups this investment and realizes an equal share of the return generated by their joint project. Cooperation is not so uniform among us. By representing it as so among contractors, however, we simplify the task of assigning them payoffs for cooperating with one another without favoring either of their available strategies over the other.

Eighth, we assume that defecting involves a contractor dividing the resources she invests in interaction equally between some joint project and preying upon her partner. We assume that if one member of a pair chooses cooperation and the other defection, the defector exploits the cooperator, seizing what she and her partner have invested in their joint project, and its entire return, for herself. And we assume that if both choose defection, neither exploits the other. Instead, each loses what she has invested in predation, recoups what she has invested in a joint project with her partner, and seizes half of the return on this project for herself.

Among us, exploiting others requires time and effort, and our assumptions about defection capture this. We assume that defectors invest some resources in cooperating with their intended victims because if cooperation is as efficient as we shall assume, doing so pays them better than simply seizing whatever their partners have invested in interaction. And the better defectors do at exploiting others, the more the faker strategy pays contractors relative to the true transformer strategy. Exploitation is not so uniform among us as these assumptions suggest. But these assumptions enable us to assign payoffs to contractors for defection, and to compare these to their payoffs for cooperation, as our project requires.

Ninth, we assume that during a representative round, being punished by a transformer enforcement mechanism involves the same consequences as being exploited by a defector. Thus, a punished contractor loses all she has invested in interacting with her partner, and realizes no return on this investment.

Our representation of transformer enforcement technology suggests that punishment should be at least so costly for contractors during a representative round. For were she removed from social cooperation permanently during a round, a defector would have no opportunity to collect a return on the resources she had invested into interacting with her partner during that round, or even to recoup these resources. And as we shall argue in specifying the payoff for being punished by a transformer enforcement mechanism, this representation of transformer punishment favors the faker over the true transformer strategy.

Tenth, and finally, we assume that a transformer enforcement mechanism never errs in punishing contractors. More specifically, we assume that every contractor punished by such an enforcement mechanism is punished for a violation she actually committed.

One might think that this assumption is incompatible with our assumption that contractors are flawed. But it is not. Institutions can be set up so that they are less prone to error than the individuals comprising them. And contractors might, as a matter of design and luck, manage to set up an enforcement mechanism which committed no errors at all during its tenure. Given our characterization of contractors, however, this is exceedingly unlikely. And even if contractors managed to set up an unerring enforcement mechanism, it would be a poor representation of the one with which we function.

Our assumption that a transformer enforcement mechanism is unerring is purely a simplifying assumption, one enabling us to define payoffs for the faker and true transformer strategies more easily. We can permissibly invoke it because an errant transformer enforcement mechanism poses the same risk to contractors whether they are cooperating or defecting, and thus the same risk to both fakers and true transformers.

Armed with these assumptions, we turn to the question of which individual strategy transformers would choose were they choosing once and for all between the faker and true transformer strategies during a representative round. Answering this question within the decision value framework, we begin by considering the maximin rule, its plausibility for our contractors, and its recommendation to them.

Maximin Reasoning

Following the *maximin rule*, contractors choose the available strategy involving the best worst outcome.

When Maximin Reasoning Is Plausible

To assign maximin reasoning a weight within the decision value framework, we must determine its plausibility within contractors' choice situation. To do so, we identify the conditions under which the maximin rule is most plausible, then determine the extent to which their choice situation satisfies these.[4]

The First Plausibility Condition for Maximin Reasoning. A choice is important when an agent stands to lose or gain a lot of utility as a result of her choice, final when she cannot reverse its effects by making another choice. By following the maximin rule, an agent minimizes her potential losses, and doing so is most plausible when she faces an important and final choice.

A contractor suited to faking who becomes a true transformer forfeits a large amount of future utility. And a contractor unsuited to faking who nonetheless becomes a faker bears a much greater risk of losing a large amount of future utility than she otherwise would. Thus, the choice between the faker and true transformer strategies is important. And, given our assumption that contractors choose once and for all between these strategies, this choice is also final.

The Second Plausibility Condition for Maximin Reasoning. The maximin rule requires an agent to bracket any information she might have, ordinal or cardinal, about the probabilities associated with the possible outcomes of her choices. But other things being equal, it is irrational for an agent to bracket reliable information she has about the possible outcomes of her choices. For an agent who brackets such information can expect her choices to be less responsive to her environment, and as a result, less effective in securing for her what she most prefers, than they would otherwise be.[5] Thus, maximin reasoning is most plausible when an agent has no reliable probability information, ordinal or cardinal, about the possible outcomes of her choices.

But our contractors each know how her personal and social characteristics compare to those of her fellows. And having jointly empowered a transformer enforcement mechanism, each knows what proportion of the violations committed each round their enforcement mechanism will punish, as well as the maximum number of fakers that can survive among them. Possessing all of this information, contractors could estimate the cardinal probabilities associated with the possible outcomes of choosing between the faker and true transformer strategies during a representative round.[6]

Like us, contractors suffer from limitations affecting their odds of realizing desired outcomes. Because they suffer from perceptual failings, contractors may overlook or mistake crucial features of their circumstances. Because they suffer from mnemonic failings, contractors may misremember or forget information. Because they suffer from cognitive failings, contractors may err in making calculations, more frequently when pressed for time or stressed. And finally, because they suffer from psychological distortions, contractors may misjudge the riskiness of particular courses of action.

To the extent that they suffer from such limitations, contractors are prone to err in executing their chosen strategies. Thus, were a contractor to disregard her limitations in estimating the cardinal probabilities associated with the possible outcomes of her choice between individual strategies, the resulting estimates would be unreliable. But as we have characterized contractors, they do not know the extent of their own limitations. Thus, they cannot generate reliable estimates of the cardinal probabilities associated with the possible outcomes of choosing between the faker and true transformer strategies during a representative round.

Let us distinguish between typical and gifted contractors. We have assumed that contractors differ in their personal and social characteristics. Certain personal and social characteristics would lend their possessors an advantage over others in evading punishment when they defect intentionally. Personal characteristics like great intelligence, for instance, would enable a defector to conceal evidence effectively, shift suspicion to others, generate consistent stories, resist interrogation, and the like. And social characteristics like great wealth or fame would enable a defector to buy off witnesses, hire private investigators, secure the best counsel in defending herself, and so on. Let us call contractors whose personal and social characteristics lend them an appreciable advantage over most of their fellows when it comes to surviving as fakers *gifted* contractors. And let us say that all other contractors are *typical* contractors.

By comparing their unreliable estimates of the cardinal probabilities associated with the possible outcomes of choosing between the faker and true transformer strategies during a representative round, every contractor can rank her odds of realizing the worst possible outcomes associated with each of these strategies. For gifted contractors, this ranking might not be reliable, but for typical contractors, it would be reliable no matter how extensive their limitations.[7] Thus, typical contractors have reliable ordinal information about the probabilities associated with the worst possible outcomes of choosing the faker and true transformer strategies during a representative round.

The Third Plausibility Condition for Maximin Reasoning.   Since maximin reasoning disregards what agents stand to gain by differentiating among the better possible outcome of a choice, it is most plausible when agents care little or nothing for such gains.

Rawls argues that this condition is satisfied when contractors choose principles of justice from behind a veil of ignorance in the original position. Knowing nothing about their preferences or starting places, argues Rawls, contractors would care much more about securing a satisfactory minimum for themselves than about acquiring more than this minimum. And according to Rawls, following the maximin rule in the original position would indeed secure contractors a basic minimum.[8]

But our contractors do not occupy the original position. Whether they would care little or nothing for what they stand to gain by differentiating among the better possible outcomes of choosing between the faker and true transformer strategies during a representative round depends crucially upon the content of their preferences. And since we have placed no restrictions on the content of contractors' preferences, we cannot be sure they would care little or nothing for such gains.

The Fourth Plausibility Condition for Maximin Reasoning. Finally, the maximin rule is most plausible when all but one of an agent's alternatives risk disaster, or when all risk disaster, but one risks a lesser disaster than others. In the first case, maximin reasoning enables an agent to avoid disaster altogether. And in the second, it enables her to minimize disaster should it befall her.

As we have defined the faker and true transformer strategies, both are probability mixtures over defection and cooperation. In cooperating, a contractor risks being exploited by her partner, with disastrous results. In defecting, a contractor risks being punished by a transformer enforcement mechanism, which also involves disastrous results. Thus, both of the alternatives available to contractors risk disaster. Indeed, both risk the very same disasters.

Maximin Reasoning Within the Decision Value Framework.

To maximize decision value, contractors must assign weights to each of maximin, disaster avoidance, and expected utility reasoning. If their choice situation satisfies few or none of the plausibility conditions for a given decision rule, contractors should assign little or no weight to it. Their choice situation satisfies only the first of four plausibility conditions for maximin reasoning, at least with respect to typical contractors. With respect to gifted contractors, it satisfies the first of these conditions, and it might satisfy the second. Thus, typical contractors should assign maximin reasoning little or no weight in choosing between the faker and true transformer strategies. It is not clear how much weight that gifted contractors should assign it in so choosing.

Conclusion

Maximin reasoning instructs contractors to choose the available strategy with the best worst outcome. But contractors must choose between the faker and the true transformer strategies, and these strategies involve precisely the same possible outcomes during a representative round. Thus, the worst outcomes of choosing the faker and true transformer strategies during a representative round are equally good (or bad) for contractors, and maximin reasoning fails to discriminate between these two strategies during such a round.

Notes

1. For a discussion of this *PD*, see the previous chapter.

2. The classical sources of this strategy are Hobbes and Hume. See Thomas Hobbes, *Leviathan*, ed. C. B. MacPherson (New York: Penguin Books, 1988), Chapter 15, and David Hume, *An Enquiry Concerning the Principles of Morals*, ed. L. A. Selby-Bigge (Oxford: Oxford University Press, 1975), 282–3. For a contemporary discussion of this strategy, see Geoffrey Sayre-McCord, "Deception and Reasons to Be Moral," *American Philosophical Quarterly* 26 (1989): 113–22.

3. For a similar representation of the choice between being moral and merely pretending to be moral, see Sayre-McCord, 185. Later, we relax the assumption that contractors are making a one-time choice among strategies, arguing that doing so does not compromise our results.

4. Here I draw heavily upon Rawls' discussion of the features of situations which lend plausibility to the maximin rule. See John Rawls, *A Theory of Justice* (Cambridge: Harvard University Press, 1971), 154–5.

5. There are environments within which this might not be so. But our community does not constitute such an environment. Thus, in the environment with which we are concerned, it is irrational for agents to disregard reliable information they have about the possible outcomes of their choices.

6. We generate such an estimate in Chapter 7.

7. For an argument to this effect, see the section of Chapter 6 entitled "The Seventh Plausibility Condition for Disaster Avoidance Reasoning."

8. For this argument, see Rawls, 154–5.

6

Disaster Avoidance Reasoning

Let us distinguish between two sorts of uncertainty. An agent chooses under *two-dimensional uncertainty* if she lacks reliable cardinal estimates for both the probabilities and the utilities associated with the possible outcomes of her choice. She chooses under *one-dimensional uncertainty* if she has reliable cardinal estimates of these utilities, but lacks reliable cardinal estimates of these probabilities. The *disaster avoidance principle* was developed to guide choice under two-dimensional uncertainty.[1]

The Disaster Avoidance Principle

Following the disaster avoidance principle, agents choose the available strategy involving the smallest probability of any disastrous outcome at all occurring, where a disastrous outcome is one entailing an unacceptably large loss of utility.

When Disaster Avoidance Reasoning Is Plausible

To assign disaster avoidance reasoning a weight within the decision value framework, we must determine its plausibility within contractors' choice situation. To do so, we identify the conditions under which the disaster avoidance principle is most plausible, then determine the extent to which their choice situation satisfies these.[2]

The First Plausibility Condition for Disaster Avoidance Reasoning.
Disaster avoidance reasoning is most plausible when all but one of an agent's alternatives risk disaster, or when all risk disasters of roughly the same magnitude.[3] In the first case, disaster avoidance reasoning, no less than maximin reasoning, assures an agent of avoiding disaster altogether. In the second case, where disaster minimization is in vain, disaster avoidance reasoning offers an agent the best hope of avoiding disaster altogether.

That the faker and true transformer strategies involve the same possible outcomes implies trivially that all of the alternatives available to transformers risk disasters of equal magnitude.

The Second Plausibility Condition for Disaster Avoidance Reasoning. Like maximin reasoning, disaster avoidance reasoning is most plausible when an agent faces an important and final choice. The disaster avoidance principle, like the maximin rule, is a conservative decision rule, most plausible when circumstances call for a conservative choice. But as we noticed in discussing maximin reasoning, the choice between the faker and true transformer strategies exhibits both of these qualities.

The Third Plausibility Condition for Disaster Avoidance Reasoning. Disaster avoidance reasoning requires an agent to bracket any information she might have about the cardinal utilities associated with the possible outcomes of her choices. But other things being equal, it is irrational for an agent to bracket reliable information she has about the possible outcomes of her choices. For an agent who brackets such information can expect her choices to be less responsive to her environment, and as a result, less effective in securing for her what she most prefers, than they would otherwise be. Thus, disaster avoidance reasoning is most plausible when an agent has no reliable information about the cardinal utilities associated with the possible outcomes of her choices.

Our contractors, however, know their own preferences. And with this information, each can determine precisely how much utility she would enjoy on each possible outcome of choosing between the faker and true transformer strategies during a representative round.

The Fourth Plausibility Condition for Disaster Avoidance Reasoning. Disaster avoidance reasoning requires an agent to disregard the non-disastrous outcomes of her choice. But if an agent stands to gain as much by realizing the right non-disastrous outcome of her choice as she stands to lose by realizing the most disastrous of its outcomes, then arguably, disregarding the non-disastrous outcomes of her choice is irrational. Thus, disaster avoidance reasoning is most plausible when the utility disparity between the non-disastrous outcomes of a choice is small relative to the utility disparity between its disastrous and non-disastrous outcomes.

The non-disastrous possible outcomes associated with choosing the faker and true transformer strategies are precisely the same during a representative round. Thus, the utility disparity between the non-disastrous outcomes associated with the alternatives available to contractors is zero.

There is, however, a significant disparity between the resource endowments associated with the disastrous and non-disastrous outcomes of choosing between the faker and true transformer strategies during a representative round.[4] And since contractors' utility payoffs increase constantly and linearly with resource endowments, there is thus a significant disparity between the utilities associated with the possible outcomes of this choice. Thus, there is a significant utility disparity between the disastrous and non-disastrous possible outcomes of choosing between the faker and true transformer strategies during a representative round.

And thus, during a representative round, the utility disparity between the non-disastrous possible outcomes of the choice between the faker and true transformer strategies is small relative to the utility disparity between the disastrous and non-disastrous possible outcomes of this choice.

The Fifth Plausibility Condition for Disaster Avoidance Reasoning. The disaster avoidance principle requires an agent to bracket any information she might have about the cardinal probabilities associated with the possible outcomes of her choices. But other things being equal, it is irrational for an agent to bracket reliable information she has about the possible outcomes of her choices, for the reasons cited above. Thus, in general, disaster avoidance reasoning is most plausible when an agent has no reliable information about the cardinal probabilities associated with the possible outcomes of her choices.

Contractors do not know the extent of their own limitations. But as we noticed in discussing maximin reasoning, without this information, they cannot generate reliable cardinal estimates of the probabilities associated with the possible outcomes of choosing the faker or true transformer strategies during a representative round.

The Sixth Plausibility Condition for Disaster Avoidance Reasoning. Where the alternatives available to an agent involve insignificantly small probabilities of disaster, agents need not worry much about avoiding disaster. Thus, disaster avoidance reasoning is most plausible when an agent's alternatives involve probabilities of disaster which are not insignificantly small.

A transformer who defects may be punished for doing so by a transformer enforcement mechanism. During a representative round, a transformer enforcement mechanism punishes between .38 and .54 of the violations committed. Typical transformers defecting during a representative round would be punished with a probability of at least .38. And even the most gifted transformers would be punished with a probability of at least .29.[5] Thus, the operation of a transformer enforcement mechanism insures that all contractors run a significant risk of disaster by defecting during a representative round.

Any contractor who cooperates may be exploited by her partner. And given their flaws, transformers would defect on their partners a significant proportion of the time no matter what proportion of them were operating as fakers. Thus, all transformers run a significant risk of disaster by cooperating during a representative round.

Since the faker and the true transformer strategies are both probability mixtures over defection and cooperation, neither involves an insignificantly small risk of disaster.

The Seventh Plausibility Condition for Disaster Avoidance Reasoning. If an agent's alternatives risk disaster with roughly equal probabilities, she can do little to avoid disaster by choosing any one of these over any other. Thus, disaster avoidance reasoning is most plausible for an agent when her alternatives involve unequal probabilities of disaster.

Cooperating, a contractor suffers disaster if her partner exploits her. Let q represent the probability that a faker would defect during any given round, and $q/4$ the probability that a true transformer would defect during any given round.[6] Given this specification of q and $q/4$, we can express the probability that a cooperator would suffer disaster during any given round as $kq + (1-k)(q/4)$.

Defecting, a contractor suffers disaster if she is punished by a transformer enforcement mechanism. A typical defector's probability of being so punished during any given round is $.38 + .62k$.

The faker strategy would involve a larger probability of disaster than the true transformer strategy for a typical contractor during any given round just in case

$$.38 + .62k > kq + (1-k)(q/4).$$

Let us assume that q approaches 1 in comparing these two payoffs, for $kq + (1-k)(q/4)$ increases relative to $.38 + .62k$ as q increases, and $0 < q < 1$.[7] Substituting .99999 for q in the above inequality, and simplifying, we find that it reduces to the claim that $k \leq 1$. But under a transformer enforcement mechanism, no more than .25 of our contractors could survive as fakers during a representative round.[8] Thus, during such a round, $k < 1$ by a considerable margin, and the faker strategy involves a larger probability of disaster than the true transformer strategy for typical contractors.

But we have not taken account of how the limitations of typical contractors affect their expectations. And one might worry that were we to do so, we would find that typical contractors' odds of suffering disaster on the faker and true transformer strategies during a representative round are equal. This is not so, however, for the following reason.

True transformers' limitations cause them to violate rules of justice accidentally. And fakers' limitations cause them to violate rules of justice, both offensively and defensively, when it is too dangerous to do so profitably. But any contractor's limitations would cause her to violate rules of justice mistakenly more frequently as a faker than as a true transformer.[9] Thus, as a typical contractor's limitations become more pronounced, her odds of suffering disaster as a faker increase relative to her odds of suffering disaster as a true transformer. And thus, however extensive their limitations, typical contractors are more likely to suffer disaster as fakers than as true transformers during a representative round.

Gifted contractors, however, are another matter. Such contractors might be just elusive enough that the faker and true transformer strategies involve equal probabilities of disaster during a representative round. And even were gifted contractors slightly more elusive than this, their limitations might equalize these probabilities. Thus, unlike typical contractors, gifted contractors might be equally likely to suffer disaster on the faker and true transformer strategies during a representative round.

The Eighth Plausibility Condition for Disaster Avoidance Reasoning. If agents could not reliably rank their odds of suffering disaster on each of their available alternatives, they could not determine which of these offered them the best odds of avoiding disaster altogether. Thus, disaster avoidance reasoning is most plausible when agents have reliable ordinal information about their odds of suffering disaster on their available alternatives.

Appealing to the argument developed in the previous section, we can rank typical contractors' odds of suffering disaster on the faker and true transformer strategies during a representative round reliably. And since typical contractors can access the information we used in developing this ranking, they can too.

Depending on how elusive they were, gifted contractors might or might not be able to rank their probabilities of suffering disaster on the faker and true transformer strategies during a representative round reliably. Were they insufficiently elusive to face lower odds of disaster as fakers than as true transformers during such a round, they could rank these probabilities reliably. And the same would be true were they so elusive as to face a lower probability of disaster as fakers than as true transformers during a representative round no matter how extensive their limitations. But gifted contractors elusive to an extent somewhere between these two extremes could not rank their odds of suffering disaster on the faker and true transformer strategies during a representative round reliably.

Disaster Avoidance Reasoning
Within the Decision Value Framework

To maximize decision value, contractors must assign weights to each of maximin, disaster avoidance, and expected utility reasoning. If their choice situation satisfies most of the plausibility conditions for a given decision rule, contractors should assign a significant positive weight to it. Their choice situation satisfies all but the third of eight plausibility conditions for disaster avoidance reasoning, at least so far as typical contractors are concerned. So far as gifted contractors are concerned, it satisfies the first, second, fourth, fifth, and sixth of these conditions, fails to satisfy the third, and might satisfy the seventh and eighth. Thus, all of our contractors, typical and gifted, should assign disaster avoidance reasoning a significant positive weight in choosing between the faker and true transformer strategies.

Conclusion

Were a contractor sufficiently gifted, she would be less likely to suffer disaster as a faker than as a true transformer during a representative round. But the operation of a transformer enforcement mechanism would limit the number of contractors who were so gifted.

Under a transformer enforcement mechanism, no more than .25 of a community's population could survive as fakers during a representative round. Let us say that each contractor managing to do so occupies a *faker niche*. During a representative round, no more than $.25N$ of a transformer community could occupy a faker niche.

To survive as a faker during a representative round is to occupy one of these niches. And to have an appreciable advantage over her fellows when it comes to surviving as a faker, a contractor must be competitive for one of these niches, must be among those most likely to win one. During a representative round, the most elusive $.25N$ members of a transformer community are the most likely to win a faker niche. Thus, during a representative round, to be gifted is to be among the $.25N$ most elusive members of a transformer community. Only these would be elusive enough to enjoy appreciably better odds than other contractors of avoiding disaster on the faker strategy. Depending on how elusive they were, such contractors might or might not face lower odds of disaster as fakers than as true transformers during a representative round.

We shall assume that all $.25N$ of the most elusive of our contractors would be so elusive as to face lower odds of disaster as fakers than as true transformers during a representative round no matter how extensive their flaws. By means of this assumption, we favor the faker over the true transformer strategy as much as our analysis permits, for were fewer of our contractors so elusive, the faker strategy would be rational for fewer of them, and the true transformer strategy rational for more of them.

Given this assumption, and our argument that typical contractors are more likely to suffer disaster as fakers than as true transformers during a representative round, disaster avoidance reasoning instructs our $.75N$ typical contractors to become true transformers during such a round, and our $.25N$ gifted contractors to become fakers.

Notes

1. The disaster avoidance principle is an invention of Greg Kavka's. For a detailed discussion of it, see Gregory S. Kavka, "Deterrence, Utility, and Rational Choice," *Theory and Decision* 12 (1980): 41–60.

2. In doing so, I draw heavily on Kavka's explication of the plausibility conditions for disaster avoidance reasoning. See Kavka, 50–1.

3. By saying that two disasters are roughly the same magnitude, I mean that the larger disaster, if there is one, involves less than twice the disutility that the smaller involves.

4. We quantify this disparity later in this chapter.

5. We assume that gifted contractors would be no less than .75 as likely as typical ones to be punished for any given violation. For a justification of this assumption, see Chapter 7.

6. In Chapter 4, we argue that fakers would defect at least four times as frequently as true transformers. As it turns out, the less frequently fakers would defect relative to true transformers, the lower their odds of suffering disaster during a representative round are relative to true transformers'. Thus, favoring the faker over the true transformer strategy as much as our analysis permits, we assume that fakers would defect four times as frequently as true transformers.

7. For an account of the range of q, see Chapter 7.

8. For an argument to this effect, see the section of Chapter 7 entitled "The Iterated Sense of Justice Game."

9. For an argument to this effect, see Chapter 4.

7

Expected Utility Reasoning

The *expected utility principle* tells agents to maximize their expected utility, but not how to do so. Maximizing expected utility is most straightforward in parametric contexts. In such contexts, the probabilities and utilities associated with the possible outcomes of an agent's choice are fixed by her environment. To maximize expected utility in a parametric context, an agent determines these utilities and these probabilities. Then, for each strategy available to her, she multiplies the utility she would realize on each of its possible outcomes by the probability of each occurring, and sums the resulting products. By choosing the strategy involving the highest such sum, an agent maximizes expected utility.

Not all choices, however, are made within parametric contexts. Agents are involved in a strategic context, or a *game*, whenever the payoffs of each depend not only on her own actions, but also on those of others.[1] To maximize her expected utility in a game, an agent must choose the strategy yielding her the most utility given the expected strategy choices of her fellows. If her fellows are expected utility maximizers, she can expect each to be doing the same as she. Under such circumstances, she should choose a strategy constitutive of an outcome on which she maximizes utility conditional on the maximizing efforts of every other agent, efforts she must assume to be similarly conditioned given her expectation that others will do the same as she. In other words, she should do what she can to realize an *equilibrium*, an outcome on which no agent has an incentive to change her strategy unilaterally.

Strategic Reasoning

This analysis suggests a reinterpretation of the expected utility principle for strategic contexts: choose a strategy which is a constituent in an equilibrium outcome (an *equilibrium strategy*). Let us call this the *strategic expected utility principle*, or for short, *strategic reasoning*.

When Strategic Reasoning Is Plausible

To assign strategic reasoning a weight within the decision value framework, we must determine its plausibility within contractors' choice situation. To do so, we identify the conditions under which strategic reasoning is most plausible, then determine the extent to which their choice
situation satisfies these.

The First Plausibility Condition for Strategic Reasoning. Strategic
reasoning was designed to guide choice within strategic contexts. In
parametric contexts, where there is no such thing as an equilibrium
strategy, it is not even clear how strategic reasoning could guide choice.
Hence, unsurprisingly, strategic reasoning is most plausible in strategic
contexts.

But contractors' choice situation is not obviously a strategic context.
After all, it contains at least one significant parametric element: a transformer enforcement mechanism. Because contractors empower such an
enforcement mechanism before selecting individual strategies, it is a
fixed feature of their environment. And because they know how it operates, each can determine how it affects the expected payoffs of her choice
between the faker and true transformer strategies. And so, within contractors' choice situation, payoffs to each are not determined solely by the
strategy choices of others.

Although it contains this parametric element, contractors' choice situation is not, strictly speaking, a parametric context. By definition, a strategic context is any context in which payoffs depend on the choices of more
than one agent. And the payoffs of the faker and true transformer strategy depend, in part, upon how many contractors choose each of these
strategies. How much each strategy pays, for instance, depends upon the
odds of encountering a faker during any given interaction, which is a
function of how many contractors choose the faker strategy. Hence, contractors' choice situation is a strategic context.

The Second Plausibility Condition for Strategic Reasoning. Strategic
reasoning is designed to guide rational agents involved in games with
other agents known to be rational. Playing against agents not known to
be rational, an agent has no reason to think that others would choose an
equilibrium strategy, so she has no reason to choose such a strategy herself. Thus, strategic reasoning is most plausible in games where the rationality of players is common knowledge.[2]

Our contractors are rational, know one another to be rational, know
one another to know one another to be rational, and so on. Hence, their
rationality is common knowledge.[3]

The Third Plausibility Condition for Strategic Reasoning. Being involved in a strategic context does not, by itself, imply the plausibility of strategic reasoning. For to reason strategically, agents must be able to identify an equilibria of the game in which they are involved. And to do so, they must have estimates of the utilities expected by each player of this game on each of its possible outcomes. Strategic reasoning is most plausible where these estimates are reliable.

Knowing her own conception of the good, each of our contractors could determine precisely how much utility she would enjoy on each of the possible outcomes of her choice between the faker and true transformer strategies.

Contractors do not know one anothers' conceptions of the good. But each can determine the resource endowments of others on each of the possible outcome of their respective choices between the faker and true transformer strategies. And given what contractors know about their circumstances, each can correlate gains and losses in resources with gains and losses in utility. Having done so, each can estimate cardinal utility payoffs for others on each of the possible outcomes of their respective choices between the faker and true transformer strategies. And, as we shall argue, for the purpose of adjudicating between these strategies by means of strategic reasoning, such estimates would be reliable.

The Fourth Plausibility Condition for Strategic Reasoning. To identify the equilibria of a game, players require not just utility estimates, but also estimates of the prior probabilities associated by each of its players with each of its possible outcomes. And again, strategic reasoning is most plausible when these estimates are reliable.

Contractors know enough about the distribution of gifts within their community and about their enforcement mechanism to estimate the cardinal probabilities of success and failure faced by each on each of their available strategies. But none knows the extent of her own limitations, or the limitations of her fellows. And without this information, contractors could not determine precisely how these would affect their expectations on the faker and true transformer strategies. For this reason, their cardinal probability estimates are not completely accurate. But as we shall argue, for the purpose of adjudicating between the faker and true transformer strategies by means of strategic reasoning, such estimates would nonetheless be reliable.

The Fifth Plausibility Condition for Strategic Reasoning. Strategic reasoning is not always plausible even when players of a game have the information required to identify its equilibria. For in some games with multiple equilibria, agents who reason strategically may find themselves playing strategies which are constituents of different equilibria. And in doing so, they may fail to maximize utility.[4] Numerous equilibrium refinements have been generated in an attempt to winnow the class of choiceworthy equilibria in games with multiple equilibria to one.[5] But none of these guarantees uniqueness of choiceworthy equilibria, so none succeeds in closing the gap between playing an equilibrium strategy and maximizing utility entirely.[6] And there is considerable controversy about which of these refinements is the most adequate. In the face of such controversy, rational agents might commit themselves to different refinements, failing to coordinate on an equilibrium as a result. For these reasons, strategic reasoning is most plausible in games containing a single equilibrium.

Once we have modelled strategy choice within contractors' choice situation as a game, we shall see that this game contains but one equilibrium.

Strategic Reasoning Within the Decision Value Framework

To maximize decision value, contractors must assign weights to each of maximin, disaster avoidance, and expected utility reasoning. If their choice situation satisfies most or all of the plausibility conditions for a given decision rule, contractors should assign a significant positive weight to it. Their choice situation satisfies all five of the plausibility conditions for strategic reasoning. Hence, contractors should assign it a significant positive weight in choosing between the faker and true transformer strategies.

The Sense of Justice Game

To determine what strategic reasoning would instruct contractors to do were they choosing between the faker and true transformer strategies during a representative round, we shall model this choice as a game, the *sense of justice game.* Then we shall imagine contractors analyzing this game for an equilibrium, and doing what strategic reasoning would instruct them to do as players of this game.

Having argued that we ought to understand contractors as choosing an individual strategy once and for all, we shall model their choice between the faker and true transformer game during a representative round as a single-play game rather than an iterated game.

The Player and Strategy Sets of the Sense of Justice Game

The player set of this game consists of all of our contractors, represented by N.

The strategy set of this game consists of the faker (F) and true transformer (TT) strategies, each of which is a probability mixture over the two moves available to contractors each round, cooperation (C) and defection (D). Let q and $q/4$ represent the probabilities that fakers and true transformers, respectively, would defect during any given round.[7] Drawing upon these terms, we can represent the faker and true transformer strategies as follows:

$$TT\!: \ (1{-}q/4)C + (q/4)D$$

$$F\!: \ (1{-}q)C + qD.$$

The Payoff Function of the Sense of Justice Game

Having so described this game's strategy set, we can define its payoff function as well. But the payoff function we shall define here is incomplete. Drawing upon our earlier distinction between typical and gifted contractors, we shall specify the payoffs of the faker and true transformer strategies only to the former. We do not specify the payoffs of these strategies to gifted contractors because our argument does not require us to do so.

The faker and true transformer strategies are probability mixtures over cooperation and defection. Thus, to specify the payoffs of these strategies, we must first specify the payoffs of their component moves. To do so, we require a precise way of talking about the probabilities and utilities comprising the expected payoffs to contractors for cooperation and defection.

Recall that k represents the proportion of a transformer community operating as fakers. So defined, k also represents a cooperator's odds of encountering a faker during any given interaction.[8] Given our earlier specification of q, kq represents a cooperator's odds of encountering a faker who will defect upon her during any given interaction. And $1{-}kq$ represents her odds of avoiding any such agent.

A transformer enforcement mechanism punishes $1{-}p$ of the violations committed each round. So defined, $1{-}p$ also represents the probability that a typical contractor who defects on her partner would be punished for doing so. And p represents the probability that a typical defector would not be so punished.

So far as the utilities associated with cooperation and defection go, let g represent the payoff to each party to mutual defection, let h represent the payoff to each party to mutual cooperation, and let i represent the payoff to a player who exploits her partner. Finally, let f represent the payoff to players who are either exploited or punished.[9]

Given the probabilities and utilities defined above, we can represent the payoffs of cooperation and defection to a contractor during any given round as follows:

$$U(C) = (1{-}kq)h + kqf$$
$$U(D) = pi + (1{-}p)f$$

We have paid cooperators h even when they cooperate with true transformers who defect on them accidentally. By so doing, we have inflated the payoff of cooperation by $(1{-}k)(q/4)(h{-}f)$.

Further, we have paid defectors i even when they defect upon true transformers and fakers defecting upon them. But each party to mutual defection loses what she has invested in predation, recoups what she has invested in a joint project with her partner, and seizes half of the return on this project for herself. And so doing, each realizes a payoff of g, with $g < i$. Thus, by paying defectors i for every defection, we have inflated the payoff for defecting on a true transformer by $p(1{-}k)(q/4)(i{-}g)$, and the payoff for defecting on a faker by $pkq(i{-}g)$.

By means of these stipulations, we render the payoffs of cooperation and defection more tractable than they would otherwise be. Within the context of our project, simplifying assumptions are acceptable just in case they favor the faker over the true transformer strategy. And these assumptions favor the faker over the true transformer strategy just in case relaxing them would require us to subtract less from the payoff of cooperation than from the payoff of defection. Hence, to justify them, we must show that

$$(1{-}k)(q/4)(h{-}f) < p(1{-}k)(q/4)(i{-}g) + pkq(i{-}g).$$

Substituting the values of f, g, h, and i into this inequality, and expressing k in terms of p, we find that this inequality reduces to the claim that $2.48 > 1$.[10] Since this claim is true, our assumptions in specifying the payoffs of cooperation and defection, taken together, favor the faker over the true transformer strategy.

Having defined payoffs for cooperation and defection, we can define the payoffs of the faker and true transformer strategies, which are just probability mixtures over these moves, to typical contractors during any given round:

$$U(F) = (1{-}q)[(1{-}kq)h + kqf] + q[pi + (1{-}p)f]$$
$$U(TT) = (1{-}q/4)[(1{-}kq)h + kqf] + q/4[pi + (1{-}p)f].$$

The Limitations of Contractors and the Payoff Function of the Sense of Justice Game. This payoff function assigns no weight to contractors' flaws in determining their payoffs on the faker and true transformer strategies. Although this is consistent with our assumption that contractors know nothing of the extent of their flaws, one might yet worry that it favors the true transformer over the faker strategy.

But as a contractor's limitations become more pronounced, she would defect more frequently on the faker strategy than on the true transformer strategy. And as we argue later in this chapter, defection always pays typical contractors less than cooperation. Thus, our disregard for typical contractors' limitations in formulating their payoffs on the faker and true transformer strategies advantages the former over the latter, as our project requires.

Suppressed Costs and the Payoff Function of the Sense of Justice Game. Contractors executing the true transformer strategy pay costs that fakers avoid, the effort involved in habituation. In defining the payoffs of the sense of justice game, we have suppressed these costs. And one might worry that in doing so, we have advantaged the true transformer over the faker strategy.

But executing the faker strategy requires contractors to pay costs that true transformers avoid. By transforming themselves, contractors effectively narrow the range of range of options they must consider carefully at any given choice point. For possessing principled preferences, an agent can rule out all unjust options at a given choice point as obviously dispreferred to any just option. Thus, at any given choice point, a true transformer calculates only the payoffs associated with her just options. Contrastingly, at any given choice point, a faker calculates the payoffs associated with both her just and unjust options. And performing such calculations involves effort. Calculating the payoffs of more options at any given choice point than true transformers, fakers would pay higher calculation costs at any given choice point than true transformers.

One might think that at any given choice point, the effort involved in self-transformation would exceed the effort fakers expend to calculate the payoffs of their unjust options. And one might think that for this reason, suppressing the costs involved in executing the faker and true transformer strategies advantages the latter over the former.

But it is not obvious that the costs of self-transformation at a choice point would always exceed the costs of calculating the payoffs associated with unjust options at that choice point. Surely this would vary with the requirements of self-transformation at a choice point and the number and complexity of unjust options at that choice point.

And even did the costs of self-transformation typically exceed the extra calculation costs involved in being a faker at any given choice point, we would not favor the true transformer over the faker strategy by suppressing these costs. For self-transformation eventually culminates in the development of principled preferences. And once contractors have developed principled preferences, executing the true transformer strategy is costless for them. Contrastingly, contractors must pay the calculation costs involved in being a faker for as long as they remain fakers. Unless habituation would cost many times more than calculating the payoffs of contractors' unjust options at any given choice point, the costs of executing the true transformer strategy would not be any higher than those of executing the faker strategy. And this contingency is ruled out by our commitment to locating contractors in a choice situation suggestive of our own circumstances. Thus, we do not advantage the true transformer over the faker strategy by suppressing the costs of executing these strategies.

The Payoff Parameters of the Sense of Justice Game

To identify the equilibrium, or equilibria, of the sense of justice game, we need to assign values to the variables in its payoff function. In specifying these values, we must satisfy three conditions. First, because we are seeking to model strategy choice within contractors' choice situation, these values should be consistent with our characterization of this situation. Second, these values should suggest conditions among us, since we seek to justify the sense of justice to members of our own community. And third, these values should advantage the faker over the true transformer strategy as much as our attempts to satisfy the first two conditions permit, so that a failure to satisfy either of these conditions would not weaken our argument for the true transformer over the faker strategy.

Consider q, which designates the probability that a given faker would defect during a given interaction. Since q is a probability, $0 \leq q \leq 1$. The value of q could not be 0. For even were all fakers to try to cooperate always, which would be irrational within a transformer community, their limitations would cause some of them to defect erroneously some of the time. And the value of q could not be 1 either, for a transformer enforcement mechanism would deter rational fakers from defecting at least some of the time. As it turns out, we need know no more about the value of q than this to identify the equilibrium of the sense of justice game.

Now consider k, which designates the proportion of transformers operating as fakers. So specified, k must also be between 0 and 1, inclusive of the endpoints of this range. To identify the equilibrium, or equilibria, of the sense of justice game, we need to know the value of k during a representative round. Under a transformer enforcement mechanism, no more than .25 of contractors could survive as fakers during a representative round.[11] Thus, during such a round, $0 \leq k \leq .25$. As it turns out, we need know no more about the value of k than this to identify the equilibrium of the sense of justice game.

Now consider the value of $1-p$, the proportion of the violations committed each round which are punished within a transformer community. As we have described a transformer enforcement mechanism, it punishes $.38 + .62k$ of the violations committed each round, so $.38 \leq 1-p \leq .54$ during a representative round.

We turn now to the utility payoffs represented by f, g, h, and i. We shall specify the values of these by analyzing how cooperation, defection, and punishment would affect each contractor's resource endowment during any given round.

At the beginning of any given round, each contractor has some endowment of resources to invest in interaction. We have assumed that each would invest all of her available resources in interaction each round. Let r_u represent each contractor's initial endowment of resources during any given round, and u the utility each associates with this endowment, the utility each would realize were she to devote all of r_u to satisfying her preferences.

A contractor exploited by her partner loses her initial endowment of resources. And given our characterization of transformer punishment, each contractor punished by a transformer enforcement mechanism for defection suffers the same loss. Let r_f represent the loss of resources suffered by each contractor exploited or punished during any given round, and recall that f represents the utility each associates with this resource loss. Then during any given round, $r_f = -r_u$, and given our assumption that utility payoffs vary in a constant and linear fashion with resource endowments, $f = -u$.

Within our community, victims of injustice often lose more than what each has invested in interaction. They are sometimes injured in ways lessening their effectiveness in future interactions. And those punished for serious injustices are often excluded from at least some future interaction, as well as forfeiting their initial resource endowments. Thus, we have specified f more conservatively than a comparison with our own circumstances would support. But in the sense of justice game, fakers are more likely to pay f than true transformers, so by specifying f conservatively, we advantage the faker over the true transformer strategy.

Let r_g represent the resource gain each contractor would realize from mutual defection, and recall that g represents the utility each would associate with this gain. Let r_h represent the resource gain each contractor would realize from cooperation during any given round, and recall that h represents the utility associated with this gain. And let r_i represent the resource gain each contractor would realize from exploiting a cooperator during any given round, and recall that i represents the utility each would associate with this gain. The values of r_g, r_h, and r_i vary with the efficiency of cooperation among contractors.

Cooperation among contractors is more efficient the larger the return each realizes on her investment of resources into cooperation. Let E represent the efficiency of cooperation among contractors, and range between 0 and infinity.[12] Given this specification of E and our characterization of mutual defection,

$$r_g = -.5r_u + .5(.5r_u + .5r_u)E.^{13}$$

Given this specification of E and our characterization of cooperation,

$$r_h = r_u E.$$

And given this specification of E and our characterization of unilateral defection,

$$r_i = -.5r_u + r_u + (.5r_u + r_u)E.^{14}$$

Thus, to quantify r_g, r_h, and r_i, we must assign a value to E.

From our assumption that contractors occupy the circumstances of justice, it follows that $E > 0$. If r_h and r_i are as we have described, and if h and i increase in a constant and linear fashion with r_h and r_i, then for typical contractors, as E increases, the payoff of cooperation increases relative to that of defection. But for all positive values of E, even the very lowest, cooperation pays typical contractors more than defection.[15] Thus, no value we might assign to E within its designated range would advantage the faker over the true transformer strategy, and we can assign E any value we like. We shall let $E = 1$, because doing so facilitates our calculations, but we could let E take any value on its range without altering the equilibrium of the sense of justice game.

If we let $E = 1$, and assume that resource endowments increase in a constant and linear fashion with utility payoffs, then $g = 0$, $h = u$, and $i = 2u$.

Among us, the amount of utility individuals derive from a unit of resources tends to decrease as their utility endowments increase. Did contractors resemble us in this respect, we would have to reduce the values of h and i, and reduce the value of i relative to h. But the higher i is relative to h, the more the faker strategy pays typical contractors relative to the true transformer strategy. Thus, by disregarding the phenomenon of diminishing marginal utility in specifying h and i, we advantage the faker over the true transformer strategy.

At this point, we have defined f, g, h, and i in terms of u, the utility each contractor associates with her initial endowment of resources during any given round. For each contractor, u is a constant. To aid us in calculating the payoffs of the faker and true transformer strategies, we shall arbitrarily assign u a value, 2 utiles.[16] If $u = 2$ utiles, then $f = -2$ utiles, $g = 0$ utiles, $h = 2$ utiles, and $i = 4$ utiles.

One might think that by specifying f, g, h, and i as constants, we imply that all contractors would realize the same amounts of utility on each of the possible outcomes of their respective strategy choices during any given round. We have not, however, assumed that what constitutes a utile is invariant between contractors. Thus, we are not committed to claiming that two contractors realizing a payoff of four utiles, for instance, enjoy the same amount of utility.

By defining f, g, h, and i as constants, we commit ourselves only to the claim that the proportional relationships among the utilities associated with the possible outcomes of choosing the faker and true transformer strategies during any given round do not vary between contractors. And the truth of this claim is implied by our characterization of cooperation and defection among contractors, and our assumptions about their interaction.

The Equilibrium of the Sense of Justice Game

In identifying the equilibrium, or equilibria, of the sense of justice game, we shall consider the choices of typical and gifted players of this game separately.

Strategic reasoning instructs typical players of the sense of justice game to choose the true transformer over the faker strategy just in case their doing so constitutes part of an equilibrium of this game. For this to be the case, the true transformer strategy must pay such players more than the faker strategy. And the true transformer strategy would pay typical players more than the faker strategy just in case cooperation would pay such players more than defection.

Substituting the values of f and h (collected in Table 7.1) into the payoff of cooperation, $(1-kq)h + kqf$, we find that it reduces to $2 - 4kq$. Substituting $.38 + .62k$ for $1-p$, and $.62 - .62k$ for p, we can express the payoff of defection, $pi + (1-p)f$, as $(.62 - .62k)i + (.38 + .62k)f$. And substituting the values of f and i (collected in Table 7.1) into this expression, we find that it reduces to $1.72 - 3.72k$.

If $q = 1$ and $k < 1$, then $2 - 4kq > 1.72 - 3.72k$. Hence, when $q = 1$, for any value of k during a representative round, the payoff of cooperation is

Table 7.1   The Values of *f*, *g*, *h*, *i*, *k*, *p*, and *q* during a Representative Round

$f = -2$	$k = [0, .25]$
$g = 0$	$p = [.46, .62]$
$h = 2$	$q = (0, 1)$
$i = 4$	

greater than or equal to the payoff of defection. But q is always less than 1 among our flawed contractors. And as the value of q decreases, the value of $2 - 4kq$ increases relative to the value of $1.72 - 3.72k$, whatever the value of k. But these claims imply that whenever $q < 1$, $2 - 4kq > 1.72 - 3.72k$. Hence, for any value of q in the range of q, and for any value of k in the range of k during a representative round, the payoff of cooperation is greater than the payoff of defection for typical players of the sense of justice game. And if cooperation pays typical players of this game more than defection for any values of q and k during a representative round, the true transformer strategy pays such players more than the faker strategy during such a round.

Gifted players, by virtue of being among the $.25N$ most elusive members of their community, would have an advantage over their typical fellows in eluding punishment for defection.[17] Favoring the faker over the true transformer strategy as much as our analysis permits, we shall assume that all gifted players are so elusive that no matter how extensive their limitations, the faker strategy would pay them more than the true transformer strategy.

Given this assumption, no gifted player choosing the faker strategy could increase her payoff by unilaterally changing strategies. And given the above argument, no typical player choosing the true transformer strategy could increase her payoff by unilaterally changing strategies. Thus, were all gifted players of the sense of justice game to choose the faker strategy and all typical players to choose the true transformer strategy, no player of this game would have an incentive to change strategies unilaterally. This outcome is an equilibrium of the sense of justice game.

Were more players than we have indicated to choose the faker strategy, the least elusive of these would not be gifted, and they would have done better to choose the true transformer strategy. And were fewer players than we have indicated to choose the faker strategy, the most elusive of these would be gifted, and would have done better to choose the faker strategy. In either of these cases, there would be at least one player of the sense of justice game with an incentive to change strategies unilaterally. And thus, this game has only the equilibrium we have described, in which the .75N typical members of a transformer community become true transformers, and the .25N gifted members of such a community become fakers.[18]

The Iterated Sense of Justice Game

In constructing the sense of justice game, we have assumed that contractors are choosing once and for all between the faker and true transformer strategies. But sometimes a just member of our community will reconsider her commitment to acting justly rather than unjustly. And sometimes unjust members of our community decide to become just. Thus, arguably, our need to represent our own circumstances accurately pushes us to conceive of contractors as choosing more than once between the faker and true transformer strategies.

Appealing to this conception of contractors, one might argue that their choice of individual strategies during a representative round is properly modelled not as the single-play sense of justice game, but as a representative round of play in an iterated variant of this game. But as a little experimentation with the prisoner's dilemma (*PD*) indicates, iterating a single-play game can change its equilibrium drastically.[19] Thus, one might argue, an appeal to the equilibrium of the single-play sense of justice game, by itself, reveals nothing about what strategic reasoning instructs our contractors to do.

To answer the *iteration objection*, we shall construct an appropriately iterated version of the sense of justice game. Then we shall argue that this game would involve precisely the same equilibrium as the single-play game, so that during a representative round of play, strategic reasoning instructs our contractors to do just what it instructs them to do in the single-play game.

Having already argued for the adequacy of the single-play game in representing our circumstances, our strategy in iterating this game is to preserve as much of its structure as we can. Accordingly, we retain its player set, its strategy set, its payoff function, and most of its payoff parameters. We alter only the ranges of k and $1-p$. Since the iterated game models interaction among contractors during some rounds which are not representative, $0 \leq k \leq 1$, and $.38 \leq 1-p \leq 1$.

But unlike the single-play game, the iterated game involves multiple rounds of interaction, with players choosing strategies anew each round. In accordance with our previous assumptions about interaction between contractors, we set no upper bound on the number of rounds in the iterated game. Instead, we shall stipulate that players of this game each participate in a finite number of rounds, but that none knows the number of rounds in which she will participate.

At the beginning of each round of the iterated game, each player chooses whichever of the faker and true transformer strategies offers her the highest payoff during that round. Then the chosen strategy of each, a probability mixture over cooperation and defection, generates her move during that round. As players move each round, their enforcement mechanism punishes $(1-p)$ of their defections, with $1-p = .38 + .62k$. After the appropriate proportion of defections has been punished, new players replace those removed from interaction, as required by our assumption that contractors inhabit a community characterized by zero population growth. Finally, the enforcement mechanism estimates the value of k and publicizes this information to new and continuing players alike.

Transformer Enforcement Within the Iterated Game

Depending on the value of k, a transformer enforcement mechanism would remove from interaction each round more fakers than true transformers, fewer fakers than true transformers, or equal numbers of fakers and true transformers. To determine the equilibrium, or equilibria, of the iterated game, we need to know when such an enforcement mechanism would punish equal numbers of fakers and true transformers.

Gifted fakers would be less likely to be punished for any given defection than other contractors would. Given the distribution of personal and social characteristics within our community, and the nature of our enforcement mechanism, it is difficult to imagine the characteristics comprising giftedness providing members of our community lacking the sense of justice with much of an advantage over others in evading punishment for injustice. But we shall assume that gifted fakers would have a substantial advantage over other contractors in this regard. In particular, we shall assume that they would be only .75 as likely as other contractors to be punished for any given defection, and that only gifted contractors would become fakers. The net effect of these assumptions is to favor the faker over the true transformer strategy by rendering fakers as difficult to punish as the requirements of our project permit.

Recall that k represents the proportion of a transformer community operating as fakers, $1-k$ the proportion of such a community operating as true transformers, and N the total population of such a community. Given that fakers would defect four times as frequently as true transformers, and that they are only .75 as likely as true transformers to be punished for any given defection, a transformer enforcement mechanism would punish equal numbers of fakers and true transformers when $(4)(.75)(kN) = (1-k)N$, that is, when $k = .25$.[20] It would punish more fakers than true transformers when $k > .25$, and more true transformers than fakers when $k < .25$.

The Equilibrium of the Iterated Game

Consider the first round of the iterated game. In the absence of a previous round upon which to base a projection of the value of k, players could not determine the precise values of p and $1-p$. And lacking this information, they could not determine precise payoffs for cooperation or defection during this round. Nonetheless, typical players have enough information to rank these payoffs in order of magnitude.

Recall, from our discussion of the single-play game, that when we substitute the values of f and h (collected in Table 7.2) into the payoffs for cooperation and defection, the former reduces to $2 - 4kq$, and the latter to $1.72 - 3.72k$.

If $q = 1$ and $k = 1$, then $2 - 4kq = 1.72 - 3.72k$. And if $q = 1$ and $k < 1$, then $2 - 4kq > 1.72 - 3.72k$. Hence, when $q = 1$, for any value of k, the payoff of cooperation is greater than or equal to the payoff of defection. But q is always less than 1 among our flawed contractors. And as the value of q decreases, the value of $2 - 4kq$ increases relative to the value of $1.72 - 3.72k$, whatever the value of k. But these claims imply that whenever $q < 1$, $2 - 4kq > 1.72 - 3.72k$. Hence, for any value of q in the range of q, and for any value of k in the range of k, the payoff of cooperation is greater than the payoff of defection for typical players of the iterated game. And if cooperation pays typical players of this game more than defection no matter what the values of k and q, the true transformer strategy offers such players a higher payoff than the faker strategy no matter what strategies their fellows choose. Thus, all typical players would choose the true transformer over the faker strategy during the first round of the iterated game.

Players of the iterated game would expect their enforcement mechanism to drive fakers within their community down to .25 of its total population eventually. But they have no way of determining how quickly it would do so prior to its operation. Thus, during the first round of play, players would not know just how many faker niches were available within their community during that round.[21] And without this informa-

Table 7.2   The Values of f, g, h, i, k, p, and q during Any Given Round of the Iterated Game

$f = -2$	$k = [0, 1]$
$g = 0$	$p = [0, .62]$
$h = 2$	$q = (0, 1)$
$i = 4$	

tion, they could not locate precisely the boundary between typical and gifted players.

A transformer enforcement mechanism, however, would always punish at least .38 of the defections occurring each round. Thus, there would never be more than .62N faker niches available within a transformer community. And this suggests a necessary condition for giftedness: to count as gifted, a contractor must be among the .62N most elusive members of a transformer community.

From this, and our argument that cooperation always pays typical players better than defection, it follows that no more than .62N players of the iterated game would choose the faker strategy during its first round. Favoring the faker over the true transformer strategy as much as our analysis permits, we shall assume that the .62N most elusive players would do so, so that during the first round of play, $k = .62$.[22] On this assumption, the remaining .38N players would become true transformers during this round.

Having chosen their strategies, players would cooperate and defect as their strategies dictated. Their enforcement mechanism would punish some proportion of those defecting.[23] By doing so, it would remove more fakers from interaction than true transformers, since $k > .25$. In this manner, it would drive k below the value determined by players' initial strategy choices. At the conclusion of the first round, the enforcement mechanism would generate an estimate of the current value of k, k_1, with $k_1 < .62$, and publicize this estimate to new and continuing players alike.[24]

Players open the second round of the iterated game by choosing strategies. True transformers surviving the first round of play would have no incentive to change strategies. The removal of some gifted fakers from interaction during the first round might render some surviving true transformers gifted enough relative to their fellows to succeed on the faker strategy. And switching to the faker strategy might maximize over the initial preferences of such contractors. But doing so would not maximize over their present preferences. For having developed principled preferences, such players most prefer to cooperate in as many of their interactions as they can. And choosing the true transformer strategy would cause them to cooperate in more interactions than choosing the faker strategy, no matter what strategies others choose. So, during the second round, surviving true transformers would reaffirm their first round strategy choice.

All other players regarding themselves as typical would choose the true transformer strategy as well. For as we argued above, typical players maximize by choosing the true transformer over the faker strategy, whatever strategies their fellows choose.

But in light of their first round play, players must reassess what is involved in being gifted and being typical. For the value of k, and thus the number of faker niches available, decreases during the first round as the result of transformer enforcement. With fewer than $.62N$ faker niches available, fewer than $.62N$ players would be competitive for these niches, so fewer than $.62N$ of them would be gifted. To determine how many players are gifted during the second round, players require an indication of how many faker niches are available at this point. The value of k_1 indicates how many faker niches were available at the end of the first round. And choosing under an enforcement mechanism designed to drive the value of k down until it reaches $.25$, players would anticipate there being no more than k_1N faker niches available by the end of the second round. Accordingly, no more than k_1N of them would choose the faker strategy during the second round.

During any round t of the iterated game, fewer than $k_{t-1}N$ players might choose the faker strategy. This would happen had some of the $k_{t-1}N$ most elusive of them already chosen the true transformer strategy, or were some not elusive enough to flourish as fakers, given their limitations. Advantaging the faker strategy over the true transformer strategy as much as our analysis permits, however, we shall disregard these possibilities. We shall assume that during any round t, none of the $k_{t-1}N$ most elusive players would be surviving true transformers. And we shall assume that all of the $k_{t-1}N$ most elusive players would be elusive enough to flourish as fakers, whatever the extent of their limitations. Given these assumptions, for any round t, the $k_{t-1}N$ most elusive players of the iterated game would choose to become fakers.

This implies that strategy choice during the second round would yield a mixture of k_1N fakers and $(1-k_1)N$ true transformers. As players moved according to their chosen strategies, their enforcement mechanism would punish $.38 + .62k_1$ of the resulting defections. Were k still above $.25$, it would again remove more fakers than true transformers from interaction. By so doing, it would drive k below the value determined by the second round strategy choices of players. At the conclusion of the second round of play, the enforcement mechanism would generate an estimate of the current value of k, k_2 with $k_2 < k_1$, and publicize this estimate.

The third round of the iterated game would resemble the second. Surviving true transformers would choose the true transformer strategy. So would all but the k_2N most elusive players, who would become fakers. The result would be a mixture of k_2N fakers and $(1-k_2)N$ true transformers. As all moved in accordance with their chosen strategies, their enforcement mechanism would punish $.38 + .62k_2$ of the resulting defections. Were k still above $.25$, it would again remove more fakers than true transformers from interaction. By doing so, it would drive k below the value determined by the third round strategy choices of players. At the conclusion of the third round of play, the enforcement mechanism would generate an estimate of the current value of k, k_3, with $k_3 < k_2$, and publicize this estimate.

Subsequently, the value of k would decline each round until the enforcement mechanism estimated the current value of k to be .25. The very next round (call it the jth round), all surviving true transformers would choose the true transformer strategy. So would all but the .25N most elusive contractors, who would become fakers. The result would be a mixture of .25N fakers and .75N true transformers. As all moved according to their chosen strategies, their enforcement mechanism would punish .38 + .62k_{j-1} of the resulting defections. For the first time during the iterated game, however, it would remove equal numbers of fakers and true transformers by doing so. As a result, k would remain at .25. At the conclusion of jth round play, the enforcement mechanism would generate an estimate of the current value of k, k_j, with $k_j = .25$, and publicize this estimate.

Subsequent rounds would proceed just as the jth round would, with k remaining at .25. Thus, during a representative round of the iterated game, .75N contractors would choose the true transformer strategy, and .25N of them would choose the faker strategy.

But this does not, by itself, answer the iteration objection. To do so, we must demonstrate that $k = .25$ is an equilibrium of the iterated game, and the only equilibrium of this game. For absent such a demonstration, we have not established that strategic reasoning would instruct our contractors to do in the iterated game just what it would instruct them to do in the single-play game. We must demonstrate, then, that when $k = .25$, no player of the iterated game would change strategies unilaterally, and that this is not the case when $k > .25$ or when $k < .25$.

During any round in which $k > .25$, the value of k, and thus the number of available faker niches, would decrease. During any such round, there would be some players just gifted enough to compete for a faker niche at round's beginning who would not be so by round's end, because some of these niches would have disappeared. The least elusive member of the kN most elusive players would be competitive for a faker niche at the beginning of any round in which $k > .25$. So such a contractor would choose the faker strategy. But the decrease in faker niches during any such round would squeeze her out of the class of those competitive for a faker niche by round's end. But as a typical player, she would have done better to choose the true transformer strategy than the faker strategy during such a round. She would, thus, have an incentive to unilaterally change strategies. Because there would exist at least one such contractor during every round of the iterated game in which $k > .25$, no such round is an equilibrium of this game.

During any round in which $k < .25$, the value of k, and thus the number of available faker niches, would increase. During any such round, there would be some players not gifted enough to compete for a faker niche at round's beginning who would be so by round's end, become some new faker niches would have appeared. The most elusive member of the $1-kN$ least elusive players would not be competitive for a faker niche at the beginning of any round in which $k < .25$. So such a player would choose the true transformer strategy. But the increase in faker niches during any such round would render her competitive for a faker niche by round's end. But as a gifted player, she would have done better to choose the faker strategy than the true transformer strategy during such a round. She would, thus, have an incentive to unilaterally change strategies. Because there would exist at least one such player during every round of the iterated game in which $k < .25$, no such round is an equilibrium of this game.

But matters are different when $k = .25$. For when $k = .25$, the number of faker niches would no longer be decreasing or increasing. During any such round, all and only those players gifted enough to compete for a faker niche at the beginning of that round would be competitive for such a niche by round's end. No player choosing the faker strategy would be rendered typical, and no player choosing the true transformer strategy would be rendered gifted. Thus, when $k = .25$, typical players would all be operating as true transformers, and gifted players would all be faking. No player would have done better to play a strategy other than the one she played during such a round. Thus, none has an incentive to unilaterally change strategies, and $k = .25$ is an equilibrium of the iterated game.

From this, it follows that the iterated game involves a single equilibrium in which the $.75N$ typical members of a transformer community become true transformers, and the $.25N$ gifted members of such a community become fakers. Thus, contrary to the iteration objection, the iterated game involves precisely the same equilibrium as the single-play game. And thus, during a representative round of play in the iterated game, strategic reasoning instructs contractors to do just what it instructs them to do in the single-play game.

Irrationality Within the Iterated Game?

On our account of the iterated game, whenever k does not equal $.25$, at least some of its players would choose strategies expected to yield less utility than other strategies available to them. One might think, however, that players seeking always to maximize utility would never choose such strategies. And one might worry that unless players of the iterated game were to choose as we have described, they would reach some equilibrium other than the one we have described, sustaining the iteration objection.

Players failing to maximize expected utility within the iterated game do so because they overlook how their enforcement mechanism affects the number of faker niches available to them each round. But given the complexity of the relationship between transformer enforcement and faker niches, and given the limitations of our contractors, it is hardly surprising that they should do so, even regularly. Thus, for some players of the iterated game to fail to maximize utility whenever k does not equal .25 is fully consistent with our description of them.

But suppose we were to replace the players of the iterated game with flawless maximizers. In the first round of play among such, the least elusive of the $.62N$ most elusive players, expecting to be squeezed out of the class of the gifted by round's end, would not fake. But their not faking exposes the next least elusive contractors to the same danger, so these would not fake either. But their not faking exposes the next least elusive contractors to the same danger, so these would not fake, and so on, until we come to the $.25N$ most elusive players. Only these could expect to remain in the class of the gifted throughout the first round. Since only gifted players of the iterated game would profit by choosing the faker strategy, only the $.25N$ most elusive players would choose the faker strategy during the first round of play under these conditions. Thus, were we to repopulate the iterated game with flawless maximizers, it would reach the equilibrium we have described after one round instead of after many. And thus, even were players of the iterated game flawless maximizers, the iteration objection would fail.

Alternative Games

The decision about whether or not to act morally is sometimes modelled in terms of the *PD*. And one might wonder why we do not model the decision about whether or not to develop and maintain the sense of justice in the same terms. If contractors must choose once and for all between strategies, what makes the single-play sense of justice game more appropriate than the single-play *PD* for modelling this choice? And if contractors must choose serially among strategies, what makes the iterated sense of justice game a better representation of this choice than the iterated *PD*?

At the first stage of their choice situation, the decision about whether or not to develop and maintain the sense of justice is a *PD*, or so we have argued. But by its second stage, contractors have empowered a transformer enforcement mechanism. Having done so, the payoffs of their available strategies are no longer determined solely by the choices of their fellows, as they are in both the single-play and the iterated *PD*. Rather, these payoffs are determined, in substantial part, by the operation of a transformer enforcement mechanism. And while both variants of the sense of justice game capture this, neither variant of the *PD* does.

"Rigged" Games

One might worry that both versions of the sense of justice game are "rigged," structured so as to yield only an equilibrium consisting mostly of true transformers.[25] But this is not so. It is not the structure of either that causes it to yield an equilibrium consisting mostly of true transformers, but the values of the variables comprising their payoffs. Were we to perturb these values in appropriate ways, both versions of the sense of justice game would yield equilibria consisting mostly or entirely of fakers.

But reflection on this feature of the sense of justice game might lead one to question its usefulness to us. For whether an appeal to either version of this game could help us to establish the rationality of maintaining the sense of justice would seem to depend entirely upon f, g, h, i, k, p, and q taking precisely the values we have specified.

Our argument does require that these terms take some values rather than others. But as a little experimentation reveals, f, g, h, i, k, p, and q need not take precisely the values we have specified for both versions of the sense of justice game to involve an equilibrium consisting mostly of true transformers.

Further, we have specified f, g, h, i, k, p, and q so as to favor the faker over the true transformer strategy as much as the requirements of our project permit. Thus, any changes to the values of these terms consistent with these requirements could only decrease the payoff of the faker strategy relative to that of the true transformer strategy. And thus, any such changes could only strengthen our argument for the rationality of maintaining the sense of justice.

A Few Words About Methodology

Our analysis of individual strategy choice among contractors owes much to formal game theory. But strategic reasoning deviates from the methodology of formal game theory in significant ways. Our agents are flawed, so that they sometimes act irrationally.[26] They are differentially endowed, so that the same strategies may promise them different pay-offs. And the games we have constructed are only partially specified, so that players of these games must choose strategies under radically incomplete information.[27]

Given the tremendous technical sophistication and explanatory success of formal game theory, however, one might wonder why we do not adopt its methodology wholesale. Why analyze the choices of contractors in terms of strategic reasoning rather than formal game theory?

While strategic reasoning is not simple, it is more simple conceptually and mathematically than formal game theory tends to be. Using strategic reasoning, we can resolve both variants of the sense of justice game with no more than the concept of a dominant strategy equilibrium and the tools provided by algebra and arithmetic. And given the nature of our project, if we can decrease the technical sophistication of our argument without compromising its representational accuracy, we should do so.

And appealing to strategic reasoning rather than to formal game theory does not compromise the representational accuracy of our argument. We are flawed agents, differentially endowed. The same strategies sometimes promise different members of our community different payoffs. And although we may each know our own expectations, and those of some others, we do not know the payoff functions of everyone with whom we interact. Strategic reasoning represents these features of our circumstances, and their implications for rational choice, more accurately than formal game theory.

We sacrifice some precision by appealing to strategic reasoning rather than formal game theory. We must say that no more than a certain proportion of contractors would become enlightened maximizers, for instance, or that the iterated game would continue for some number of rounds before reaching its equilibrium. But this sacrifice has not prevented us from deriving results which are precise enough for our purposes. And in the context of our project, this sacrifice pays off, yielding an argument for the rationality of maintaining the sense of justice more accessible to members of our community, and more sensitive to their actual circumstances, than it would otherwise be.

Conclusion

Expected utility reasoning instructs agents to play a strategy comprising an equilibria of any game in which they find themselves. We have argued that the single-play sense of justice game involves a single equilibrium. And we have argued that were we to iterate the sense of justice game, so as to represent our own circumstances more accurately, it would involve precisely the same equilibrium during a representative round of play. Thus, whether we represent contractors' choices of individual strategies during a representative round in terms of the single-play game, or in terms of a representative round of the iterated game, expected utility reasoning instructs them to choose in the same way. The .75N typical members of a transformer community should become true transformers, and the .25N gifted members of such a community should become fakers.

Notes

1. This is how K. Binmore and P. Dasgupta define games in their seminal text on game theory. See K. Binmore and P. Dasgup, *Economic Organizations as Games* (New York: Basil Blackwell Press, 1986), 1.

2. For a detailed discussion of this common knowledge condition, see David Lewis, *Convention: A Philosophical Study* (Cambridge: Harvard University Press, 1969), 52–60.

3. Common knowledge of rationality follows from our assumption that contractors are rational conjoined with our assumption that each knows how her personal characteristics compare with those of her fellows.

4. The game of chicken provides a fairly spectacular example of such a game. For a discussion of how players of chicken may fail to maximize by playing an equilibrium strategy, see Brian Skyrms, *The Dynamics of Rational Deliberation* (Cambridge: Harvard University Press, 1990), 18–9.

5. See, for example, the discussion of *perfect* equilibria in Reinhard Selten, "Re-examination of the Perfectness Concept for Equilibrium Points in Extensive Games," *International Journal of Game Theory* 4 (1975): 25–35. Or see the discussion of *proper* equilibria in R. Myerson, "Refinements of the Nash Equilibrium Concept," *International Journal of Game Theory* 7 (1978): 73–80.

6. For illustrations of the failure of several prominent equilibrium refinements to close this gap, see Skyrms, 20–6.

7. In Chapter 4, we argue that fakers would defect at least four times as frequently as true transformers. As it turns out, the less frequently fakers would defect relative to true transformers, the less the faker strategy pays typical contractors relative to what the true transformer strategy pays them. Thus, favoring the faker over the true transformer strategy as much as our analysis permits, we assume that fakers would defect four times as frequently as true transformers.

8. Do not confuse cooperators and defectors with true transformers and fakers. The former pair of terms describes agents in terms of their moves during a round, the latter, in terms of their dispositions. Both fakers and true transformers are cooperators at some times, defectors at others.

9. For a justification of the assumption that being exploited and being punished would involve the same payoff, see Chapter 5.

10. For the values of f, g, h, and i, derived later in this chapter, see Table 7.1 or Table 7.2. Since $1-p = .38 + .62k$, we can express k as $1 - p/.62$.

11. For an argument to this effect, see the section of this chapter entitled "The Iterated Sense of Justice Game."

12. Thus, when $E = .5$, cooperation pays contractors a 50% yield. When $E = 1$, cooperation pays contractors a 100% yield. When $E = 2$, cooperation pays contractors a 200% yield. And so on.

13. Exploiting a defector during any given round, a defector expends half of her initial resource endowment on predation $(-.5r_u)$, recoups what she has invested in a joint project with her partner (for no net loss or gain), and seizes half of the return on this project for herself $.5(.5r_u + .5r_u)(E)$.

14. Exploiting a cooperator during any given round, a defector expends half of her initial resource endowment on predation $(-.5r_u)$, and seizes what her partner has invested in their joint project (r_u), and the entire return on this joint project $(.5r_u + r_u)(E)$, for herself.

15. Expressing p in terms of k, cooperation pays typical contractors more than defection when $(1-kq)h + kqf > (.62 - .62k)i + (.38 + .62k)f$. Converting f, h, and i into their associated resource endowments, we can express this claim as $(1-kq)r_u E + kq(-r_u) > (.62 - .62k)[.5r_u + (.5r_u + r_u)E] + (.38 + .62k)(-r_u)$. As E approaches 0, the payoff of cooperation approaches $-kqr_u$ and the payoff of defection approaches $-.07r_u - .93kr_u$. Converting these resource endowments back into their associated utility payoffs, as E approaches 0, the payoff of cooperation approaches $-kqu$ and that of defection approaches $-.07u - .93ku$. Thus, cooperation pays typical contractors more than defection as E approaches 0 just in case $-kqu > -.07u - .93ku$, or simplifying, just in case $q < .07/k + .93$. But this inequality is true no matter what value k takes within its designated range. Thus, no matter how low the value of E, cooperation pays typical contractors more than defection.

16. A *utile* is a unit of utility.

17. For an argument that to be gifted during a representative round is to be among the $.25N$ most elusive members of a transformer community, see Chapter 6.

18. And, as we have promised, this reveals that contractors' choice situation satisfies the fifth plausibility condition for strategic reasoning.

19. For one account of such experimentation, see Robert Axelrod, *The Evolution of Cooperation* (New York: Basic Books, Inc., 1984), 27–54.

20. We argue that fakers would defect four times as frequently as true transformers in Chapter 4.

21. For the concept of a faker niche, see Chapter 6.

22. If fewer did so, a transformer enforcement mechanism would drive k down to .25, and play within the iterated game to the equilibrium for which I shall argue, even more quickly than I shall describe.

23. Having no previous estimate of k from which to work, a transformer enforcement mechanism must somehow assign k a value between 0 and 1 during the first round. It might do so by duplicating our reasoning about the value of k during the first round, by using a randomizing device, or by some other method. For our purposes, neither the value a transformer enforcement mechanism assigns to k during the first round, nor its method for doing so, matter. For this value affects only the number of rounds required for the iterated game to reach its equilibrium, and not the nature of this equilibrium.

24. The subscript on k indicates that it is an estimate of the value of k at the end of some particular round, with the value of this subscript indicating the round for which subscripted k is an estimate. In this manner, we distinguish estimates of the value of k from the actual value of k, as necessitated by the different roles played by each in the iterated game. Estimates of the value of k guide the strategy choices of contractors each round, and determine the effectiveness of their enforcement mechanism. The actual value of k determines the relative rates at which contractors choosing the faker and true transformer strategies are punished each round.

25. I thank E. F. McClennen for raising this worry.

26. Others have treated the possibility of irrational choice by agents more formally. See, for instance, Selten, 25–55.

27. Others have treated games of incomplete information more formally. See, for example, John Harsanyi, "Games with Incomplete Information Played by 'Bayesian' Players, Parts I, II, and III," *Management Science* 14 (1967): 159–82, 320–34, 486–502.

8

The Individual Rationality
of Self-Transformation

Having discussed the relative plausibility of maximin, disaster avoidance, and expected utility reasoning within contractors' choice situation, and what each would recommend to our contractors during a representative round, we invoke the decision value framework to reconcile these recommendations.

Let W_m, W_d and W_e represent subjective weights assigned by agents to maximin, disaster avoidance, and expected utility reasoning, respectively. Let $UBWO(A)$ represent the utility associated with the best worst outcome of a given act, A. Let PAD represent the probability of an agent avoiding disaster if she chooses A. And let $EU(A)$ represent the expected utility associated with A. We define the decision value of A as follows:

$$DV(A) = W_m \times UBWO(A) + W_d \times PAD(A) + W_e \times EU(A).$$

We have assumed that under conditions of uncertainty, instrumentally rational agents would maximize decision value.

Decision Values of the Faker and True Transformer Strategies

Given this assumption, contractors would select whichever of the faker and true transformer strategies has the highest decision value associated with it. So consider the decision values of the faker and true transformer strategies, $DV(F)$ and $DV(TT)$, during a representative round.

Contractors' choice situation satisfies hardly any of the plausibility conditions for maximin, at least so far as typical contractors are concerned. Thus, typical contractors should assign a very low value to W_m in choosing between the faker and true transformer strategies. Gifted contractors may find that their choice situation satisfies as many as half of the plausibility conditions for maximin. Thus, it is not clear what value gifted contractors should assign to W_m in choosing an individual strategy. But to determine what maximizes decision value for contractors during a representative round, we do not need to know anything about the magnitude of the values that contractors should assign to W_m in choosing an individual strategy. For since the faker and true transformer strategies are probability mixes over the same two actions, both involve the very same best worst outcome during any given round. Thus, for both typical and gifted contractors during a representative round,

$$W_m \times UBWO(F) = W_m \times UBWO(TT).$$

Contractors' choice situation satisfies most of the plausibility conditions for disaster avoidance reasoning, so that contractors should assign a significant positive value to W_d in choosing between the faker and true transformer strategies. And a typical contractor is more likely to avoid disaster as a true transformer than as a faker during a representative round, or so we have argued. Thus, for typical contractors during such a round,

$$W_d \times PAD(TT) > W_d \times PAD(F).$$

Contractors' choice situation satisfies most of the plausibility conditions for expected utility reasoning, so that contractors should assign a significant positive value to W_e in choosing between the faker and true transformer strategies. And a typical contractor can expect more utility as a true transformer than as a faker during a representative round, or so we have argued. Thus, for typical contractors during such a round,

$$W_e \times EU(TT) > W_e \times EU(F).$$

But these three claims, taken together, imply that for typical contractors during a representative round,

$$DV(TT) > DV(F).$$

And given our assumption that gifted contractors are elusive enough so that during a representative round

$$W_d \times PAD(F) > W_d \times PAD(TT) \text{ and } W_e \times EU(F) > W_e \times EU(TT),$$

it follows that for such contractors during such a round,

$$DV(F) > DV(TT).$$

Maximizing Decision Value

These claims imply that choosing individual strategies during a representative round, all typical contractors maximize decision value by becoming true transformers, and all gifted contractors do so by becoming fakers. Thus, were our contractors to maximize decision value during a representative round, the result would be a transformer community consisting of $.75N$ true transformers and $.25N$ fakers. And since contractors are opaque, what maximizes decision value for them during a representative round maximizes decision value for them over their cooperative lifetimes.

Erroneous Strategy Choices

One might worry that the limitations of contractors would cause some to err in choosing once and for all between their available strategies. As a result of such errors, less than $.75N$ of them might choose the true transformer over the faker strategy, undercutting our conclusion that maximizing decision value, all but the $.25N$ most elusive of our contractors would become true transformers.

When it comes to justifying the sense of justice to individuals, however, what matters most is what our flawed contractors would do were they doing as they should, not what they would do in error. And our argument implies that $.75N$ of our flawed contractors would choose the true transformer over the faker strategy were they doing as they should. Thus, were fewer than $.75N$ of them to become true transformers due to the errors of some in maximizing decision value, this would not compromise our justification of the sense of justice.

One might yet worry that if contractors could expect their errors to result in significantly fewer than $.75N$ of them becoming true transformers, our argument that typical contractors maximize decision value by becoming true transformers would be compromised. But this argument would not be compromised even could contractors expect significantly fewer than $.75$ of their number to become true transformers, for the true transformer strategy maximizes decision value for typical contractors no matter what value k takes within its designated range. And besides, contractors cannot expect their errors to reduce significantly the proportion of their number becoming true transformers, for their flaws are such as to cause errors favoring neither of their available strategies over the other.

Thus, they can expect their errors in choosing once and for all between the faker and true transformer strategies to cancel one another out, with no net effect on the outcome of this choice.

Enlightened Maximizers

We have described contractors as choosing between the faker and true transformer strategies. But consider a third strategy that they might opt for: the *enlightened maximizer strategy*. Enlightened maximizers do not develop the sense of justice. Like fakers, they remain willing to defect whenever they expect to maximize on their initial preferences by doing so. But like true transformers, they seek to limit the risk of punishment to which their flaws expose them. To limit this risk, enlightened maximizers develop the following habit: whenever tempted to defect, each reminds herself of her flaws, and of the cautionary arguments against defecting which appeal to these flaws. By so doing, each develops a cognitive brake on her tendency to act unjustly, rather than the conative brake developed by true transformers.

Arguably, under a transformer enforcement mechanism, an enlightened maximizer would choose cooperation and defection with precisely the same frequency as a true transformer. For a contractor's very reasons for becoming a true transformer would provide her with equally good reasons against defecting whenever tempted to do so as an enlightened maximizer. And if these reasons would convince a contractor to become a true transformer, then they should convince her not to defect as an enlightened maximizer.

But if true transformers and enlightened maximizers would be behaviorally indistinguishable, then neither disaster avoidance nor expected utility reasoning could distinguish between these strategies. And this implies that were we to make the enlightened maximizer strategy available to contractors, none would have to become true transformers to maximize decision value.[1] Since there is no principled reason for excluding this strategy from contractors' choice situation, the success of our argument that most would become true transformers would seem to depend on our arbitrarily restricting the strategies available to them.[2]

But note that enlightened maximizers, like fakers and true transformers, must choose each round between cooperation and defection. And this means that we can understand enlightened maximizers as contractors who follow a strategy which, like the faker and true transformer strategies, is a probability mixture over cooperation and defection. So understood, the enlightened maximizer strategy would issue in the same behavior as the true transformer strategy just in case both involved the same probability mixture over cooperation and defection.

True transformers precommit themselves to cooperation, insofar as they can do so. By developing the sense of justice, they render themselves incapable of defecting intentionally during an interaction, at least insofar as they are rational. Having done so, true transformers defect during an interaction only if they somehow err in applying rules of justice. None of the other types of error to which flawed contractors are susceptible can bring true transformers to defect.[3]

Enlightened maximizers, contrastingly, defect any time doing so promises them more than cooperating, taking into account all cautionary arguments against defection. All of the errors which might cause true transformers to defect might cause enlightened maximizers to defect as well. Unlike true transformers, however, enlightened maximizers might also defect because they have overestimated the potential gains associated with doing so. Or they might overestimate their odds of being exploited during an interaction, and defect defensively. Or they might defect because they have underestimated their odds of being punished during a particular interaction.

Indeed, errors of all of these types would cause enlightened maximizers to defect at least some of the time. For even if contractors could reduce the frequency of such erroneous defections by reviewing the cautionary arguments against defecting whenever tempted to do so, their flaws prevent them from eliminating such defections in this manner. Thus, enlightened maximizers would defect erroneously under all of the same circumstances as true transformers, and then some. And thus, enlightened maximizers would defect more frequently, and cooperate less frequently, than true transformers.

Because the enlightened maximizer and true transformer strategies involve different probability mixtures over cooperation and defection, they would issue in different patterns of behavior. Thus, the objection that disaster avoidance and expected utility reasoning could not distinguish between these two strategies because they involve identical patterns of behavior is mistaken. And thus, merely making the enlightened maximizer strategy available within contractors' choice situation does not falsify our argument that most of them would become true transformers.

An Enlightened Maximizer Invasion?

But even if the enlightened maximizer strategy is distinct from the true transformer strategy, it might yet be able to invade a transformer community. And if enough of our contractors would become enlightened maximizers were this strategy available to them, we could sustain our conclusion that most would become true transformers only by arbitrarily restricting their available strategies.

The enlightened maximizer strategy could invade a transformer community only were it distinct from both the faker and the true transformer strategies. We have argued for its distinctness from the true transformer strategy. As we have described fakers, however, they consider all of the reasons for and against defection before defecting in a particular instance, including those deriving from their flaws. And it is not clear that developing the habit of rehearsing some of these reasons would yield a mode of choice appreciably different from the one exhibited by fakers, at least not among contractors flawed as we are and choosing under circumstances like our own.

But suppose the enlightened maximizer strategy were distinct from the faker strategy among such contractors. Even in this case, one of our contractors would choose the enlightened maximizer strategy only if it paid her no less than the higher-paying of the faker and true transformer strategies.

Our argument for the distinctness of the enlightened maximizer and true transformer strategies implies that the former involves a lower decision value for typical contractors than the latter. For the enlightened maximizer strategy weights defection higher, and cooperation lower, than the true transformer strategy. And we have argued that cooperation always pays typical contractors more than defection, whether we are comparing payoffs by means of disaster avoidance or expected utility reasoning. Thus, no typical contractors would become enlightened maximizers.

Nor do gifted contractors seem to have an incentive to adopt the enlightened maximizer over the faker strategy. For any given contractor would either be gifted enough for defection to involve a lower probability of disaster and a higher expected payoff for her than cooperation, or not. Were a contractor so gifted, then the faker strategy, assigning defection a higher probability than the enlightened maximizer strategy, would maximize decision value for her. And were she not so gifted, the true transformer strategy, assigning a higher probability to cooperation than the enlightened maximizer strategy, would yield her the highest decision value. It would seem, then, that gifted transformers would not become enlightened maximizers either.

But this is too fast, for we have neglected contractors just elusive enough for cooperation and defection to involve equal probabilities of disaster and equal expected payoffs. For those on this cusp, call them *cuspers*, the enlightened maximizer strategy would be a rational strategy, though no more or less so than the faker or true transformer strategies.

Cuspers would have no reason to choose any one of these three strategies over any other. Assuming that rational contractors would randomize in choosing among equirational strategies, cuspers would choose the faker strategy .33 of the time, the enlightened maximizer strategy .33 of the time, and the true transformer strategy .33 of the time.[4] Assuming that at least some of our contractors are cuspers, at least some would become enlightened maximizers, were this option available to them. And the more contractors that would become enlightened maximizers, the fewer would become true transformers or fakers.

Being neither typical nor gifted, cuspers are among neither the .38N least elusive, nor the .25N most elusive, of contractors. Randomizing among the faker, true transformer, and enlightened maximizer strategies, .33 of any cuspers among contractors would become enlightened maximizers. And of these, .5 would have become true transformers, and .5 fakers, were they choosing strategies in the absence of the enlightened maximizer strategy.[5] Thus, of the no more than .37N cuspers among contractors, only .33 would choose the enlightened maximizer strategy were it available to them, and only .5 of these would have become true transformers in contractors' original choice situation. And thus, were we to make the enlightened maximizer strategy available to contractors, no more than .06N fewer of them would become true transformers than would were they choosing between the faker and true transformer strategies alone.

In the worst-case scenario for our project, choice among the faker, true transformer, and enlightened maximizer strategies by contractors would yield an outcome consisting of .19N fakers, .69N true transformers, and .12N enlightened maximizers. This three-way split would not sustain our argument that .75N of our contractors would become true transformers. It would, however, sustain an argument that .69N of them would do so.

Any retreat from the claim that .75N of our contractors would become true transformers would force us to weaken our conclusion about how many of us are rationally required to maintain the sense of justice. But we would have to retreat from the claim that .75N of our contractors would become true transformers only if, despite our suggestions to the contrary, the enlightened maximizer strategy were distinct from the faker strategy among our contractors. And we would have to retreat all the way to the claim that .69N of our contractors would become true transformers only if cuspers would constitute .37N of our contractors, exhibiting a much lumpier distribution of personal and social characteristics than we do.

Suppose that cuspers constituted a more modest .1N of our contractors, still an exaggeration of the cusper population within our own community given the distribution of personal and social characteristics therein. In this case, making the enlightened maximizer strategy available to contractors would result in only .017N fewer of them becoming true transformers than would do so were they choosing between the faker and true transformer strategies alone.[6] And more modest representations of the cusper population among contractors would yield even smaller reductions in the number of contractors choosing the true transformer strategy.

Thus, were we to make the enlightened maximizer strategy available to contractors, fewer than .75N of them might choose the true transformer strategy. But in a choice situation representing our own circumstances accurately, very nearly .75N of them would do so. And as we shall see, whether rationality requires precisely .75N of our contractors to become true transformers, or very nearly .75N of them to do so, makes no appreciable difference when it comes to the success or failure of our project.

The Decision Value Framework and Justification

One might worry that the decision value framework is too idiosyncratic and controversial an account of substantive rationality to ground a successful justification of the sense of justice. But while reliance on the decision value framework enables us to update our argument for the rationality of the sense of justice at any time to include appeals to new decision rules, this argument does not itself presuppose the general adequacy of the decision value framework as an account of substantive rationality. For we can show anyone who accepts the adequacy of our short list of decision rules for rational choice under uncertainty that all but the .25N or so most elusive of our contractors would become true transformers without invoking the decision value framework at all.

To do so, we need only appeal to our earlier treatments of maximin, disaster avoidance, and expected utility reasoning. We have argued that given their circumstances, maximin reasoning is implausible for typical contractors. And we have argued that disaster avoidance and expected utility reasoning, both plausible for typical contractors, recommend that all such contractors choose the true transformer over the faker and enlightened maximizer strategies. Given that rational agents would follow only the recommendations of decision rules which are plausible for them, and given the adequacy of our short list of rules, these arguments imply that all but the .25N or so most elusive of our contractors would become true transformers.

But this argument appeals to the claim that maximin reasoning is implausible for typical contractors while disaster avoidance and expected utility reasoning are plausible for them. And one might worry about the support we have offered for this claim. For although we have identified plausibility conditions for each of these decision rules, and analyzed the extent to which contractors' choice situation satisfies these conditions, one might doubt that we have articulated anything like a common measure expressing the plausibility of these rules. Absent such a measure, we can determine nothing about the relative plausibility of these rules for any of our contractors.[7]

But we have articulated a common measure for comparing the plausibility of different decision rules, albeit a rough one. Different decision rules for choice under uncertainty have been developed to guide choice in different contexts. We determine the plausibility of any such decision rule for an agent by comparing her choice situation to the context for which that rule was developed. A given decision rule is plausible for an agent if her choice situation resembles this context closely, implausible if it bears little or no resemblance to it. And the plausibility conditions of maximin, disaster avoidance, and expected utility reasoning provide a rough measure of a given choice situation's resemblance to the context for which each of these rules was developed.

An appeal to this measure sustains the claim that disaster avoidance and expected utility reasoning are plausible for typical contractors, while maximin reasoning is implausible for them. And by appealing to this claim, we can sustain the conclusion that all but the $.25N$ or so most elusive of our contractors would become true transformers without invoking the decision value framework. Thus, our argument for the rationality of the sense of justice does not presuppose the adequacy of the decision value framework as a general account of substantive rationality.

Conclusion

In this chapter, we have argued that to maximize decision value at the second stage of their choice situation, all but the $.25N$ or so most elusive of our contractors must become true transformers at this stage. Given the assumptions of our analysis, this implies that approximately $.75N$ of our contractors would choose the true transformer over the faker strategy at the second stage of their choice situation. And this implies that self-transformation is individually rational for approximately $.75N$ of our contractors.

An appeal to this argument, in conjunction with an appeal to the argument developed in Chapter 4, constitutes a fundamental justification of the sense of justice for all typical members of our community, for all but the most elusive $.25$ of so of them. Whether we have any hope of extending this justification to cover gifted members of our community is a matter we shall take up in the final chapter of this book.

Notes

1. By appealing to the costs involved in developing habits of justice, one might argue the stronger claim that contractors maximize decision value by be-

coming enlightened maximizers rather than true transformers. But becoming an enlightened maximizer requires a contractor to develop habits as well, for instance, the habit of rehearsing the arguments against defection each time she considers defecting. And there is no reason to think that developing such habits would be less costly than developing habits of justice.

2. I thank Duncan MacIntosh for suggesting this objection to me.

3. For an account of these errors, see Chapter 4.

4. For a discussion of some difficulties associated with this assumption, see Duncan MacIntosh, "Buridan and the Circumstances of Justice (On the Implications of the Rational Unsolvability of Certain Co-ordination Problems)," *Pacific Philosophical Quarterly* 73 (1992): 150–73.

5. Were cuspers choosing between the faker and true transformer strategies alone, they would randomize, choosing each with a probability of .5.

6. $(.33)(.1N)(.5) = .0165N$.

7. I owe this objection to Duncan MacIntosh.

9

Toward an Account of
Rational Preference Revision

We have argued that rationality requires our contractors to transform themselves by altering their intrinsic preferences. But orthodox accounts of rationality typically assume that agents cannot alter their intrinsic preferences. For on such accounts, intrinsic preferences are given to agents by their environment, not chosen. And not being chosen by agents, intrinsic preferences are subject neither to rational assessment nor revision.

Were this the case, the conclusions of the last chapter would be seriously undermined. For the principle of ought implies can applies to rational obligation no less than to moral obligation. Thus, were it impossible for rational agents to revise their intrinsic preferences, we would be mistaken in claiming that our shallowly rational contractors ought to do so.

Taking a cue from actual individuals, we have supposed that our shallowly rational contractors could revise their intrinsic preferences over actions through habituation.[1] And given our concern that contractors reflect the capacities of actual individuals, this is appropriate. But the claim that a shallowly rational agent could revise her intrinsic preferences over actions through habituation involves a paradox.[2]

Let X and Y be mutually exclusive actions, and consider a shallowly rational agent who prefers X to Y, instrumentally or intrinsically. To acquire an intrinsic preference for y over x by means of habituation, such an agent would have to repeatedly Y when she could X. But preferring X to Y, it would be irrational for her to y when she could X, for so doing would prevent her maximizing over her preferences. Thus, it appears that an shallowly agent preferring X to Y could habituate herself into an intrinsic preference for Y over X only by acting irrationally, at which point she would cease to be a shallowly rational agent.[3]

Initially, contractors prefer instrumentally acting unjustly to acting justly. But in transforming themselves, they develop an intrinsic preference for acting justly over acting unjustly. Thus, what we have been supposing all along, that our shallowly rational contractors could transform themselves by means of habituation, appears self-contradictory.

To salvage this supposition, we must dispel this paradox. We do so by developing a habituation model of rational preference revision, then appealing to this model to establish that it is logically possible for our shallowly rational contractors to habituate themselves into principled preferences.

The Habituation Model of Rational Preference Revision

The guiding idea of the habituation model is the idea that the causality between preferences and action works both ways.[4] An agent's preferences determine her actions, and her actions, at least in part, determine what preferences that she has. But to explain precisely how an agent can revise her intrinsic preferences through habituation without acting irrationally, we must appeal to a particular psychology.

The Psychology Assumed by the Habituation Model

The components of the psychology we shall assume are as follows.

First, agents realize a feeling of satisfaction from satisfying their intrinsic preferences (among other things). And they realize more of this feeling from doing so the more extensively they satisfy their intrinsic preferences.

Second, agents realize derivative satisfaction from doing what they perceive as contributing to the eventual satisfaction of their intrinsic preferences. They realize more derivative satisfaction from actions the more extensively they perceive these as contributing to the satisfaction of their intrinsic preferences. And perceiving increased facility at such actions as contributing more to the satisfaction of their intrinsic preferences, they realize more derivative satisfaction from such actions the better they become at them.

Third, agents prefer intrinsically feeling more satisfaction, whatever its source, to feeling less. And they rank satisfying this preference highly, more highly than they rank satisfying any of their particular preferences over actions, intrinsic or instrumental.[5]

Fourth, agents can come to find satisfying in themselves activities once yielding them only derivative satisfaction. Repeatedly realizing derivative satisfaction from an activity, an agent will begin to associate this activity with feeling satisfied. Over time, through such nonrational association, she will come to take satisfaction in the mere performance of the activity. That is, she will eventually come to find it intrinsically satisfying, and to roughly the same extent she found it derivatively satisfying.[6]

And fifth, agents believe in the general effectiveness of habituation as a means of preference revision. More precisely, they believe that if an agent repeatedly does X rather than Y with the intention of developing an intrinsic preference for X over Y, then she is likely to end up with such a preference.[7]

Preference Revision Through Habituation

Let X and Y be mutually exclusive actions, and consider a shallowly rational agent preferring X over Y, instrumentally or intrinsically, who must come to prefer Y over X intrinsically to maximize over her present preferences.

Given the above psychology, such an agent could acquire an intrinsic preference for Y over X in two steps. The first step is cognitive: she must analyze her circumstances. If, upon doing so, she were to realize that she requires an intrinsic preference for Y over X to maximize on her present preferences, then because she is a flawless maximizer, she would prefer instrumentally to prefer intrinsically Y to X. The second step is practical: she must repeatedly Y instead of X because she prefers instrumentally to prefer intrinsically Y to X. Doing so enough times would, under the right conditions, yield an intrinsic preference for Y over X.

Why should this be so? An agent who prefers instrumentally to prefer intrinsically Y to X would realize derivative satisfaction from Y-ing when she could X, because she would perceive herself as contributing to the satisfaction of one or more of her intrinsic preferences by so doing.[8] If she would realize more derivative satisfaction from Y-ing than she would satisfaction from X-ing, then she would Y instead of X.[9] As she did, she would become better at Y-ing. As she got better at Y-ing, she would realize more derivative satisfaction from Y-ing when she could X. Preferring to feel more such satisfaction rather than less, she would be motivated to Y instead of X more often.[10] As a result, she would get even better at Y-ing, so that she would realize even more derivative satisfaction from Y-ing when she could X, which would motivate her to Y when she could X even more often, and so on. This cycle would continue until the agent involved either ceased to improve at Y-ing, or the preference driving habituation (an instrumental preference to prefer intrinsically Y to X) was satisfied.

Over the course of such habituation, association would gradually convert the derivative satisfaction such an agent would take in Y-ing when she could X into intrinsic satisfaction. At some point during this conversion, she would take more intrinsic satisfaction in Y-ing when she could X than she would take in X-ing when she could Y. One of the (unexceptional) ways an agent could acquire an intrinsic preference for Y over X is to discover that Y and X are of a kind with W and V when she already has an intrinsic preference for W over V.[11] Realizing that Y-ing rather than X-ing is (now) of a kind with feeling more satisfaction rather than less, for which she already has an intrinsic preference, such an agent would prefer intrinsically Y to X. At this point, having brought herself from preferring to prefer intrinsically Y to X to preferring intrinsically Y to X, such an agent would have successfully revised her intrinsic preferences through habituation.

On this model of preference revision, habituation does not require an agent to perform actions satisfying none of her preferences. Nor does it require her to perform actions satisfying her preferences to a lesser degree than other actions available to her. Thus, an appeal to this model establishes that a shallowly rational agent preferring X to Y, instrumentally or intrinsically, could develop an intrinsic preference for Y over X by means of habituation.

More importantly, at least for our purposes, such an appeal establishes that our shallowly rational contractors could develop principled preferences through habituation. Analyzing her circumstances, each would realize that to maximize over her initial preferences, she must convert her instrumental preference for acting unjustly rather than justly into an intrinsic preference for doing so. And being rational, each would prefer instrumentally to so revise her intrinsic preferences. Endowed with the above psychology, a contractor who repeatedly acted justly rather than unjustly because she preferred instrumentally to prefer intrinsically acting justly to acting unjustly would eventually develop principled preferences.

Fakers and Habituation

On the habituation model, contractors develop principled preferences by repeatedly acting justly rather than unjustly. But the fakers in a transformer community must repeatedly act justly rather than unjustly to avoid being punished by a transformer enforcement mechanism. Thus, it appears that on the habituation model, fakers would develop principled preferences in the course of avoiding their community's enforcement mechanism. And a community in which no one lacks the sense of justice bears little resemblance to our own community.

But we have not claimed that all contractors would develop principled preferences if they repeatedly acted justly rather than unjustly. Rather, we have claimed that so acting would cause contractors who have an instrumental preference to develop principled preferences to develop such preferences. Lacking such preferences, fakers would not see themselves as satisfying any of their preferences by acting justly rather than unjustly, so they would not realize any derivative satisfaction from so acting. And not realizing any derivative satisfaction from acting justly rather than unjustly, fakers could not develop principled preferences in the manner depicted by the habituation model.

Habituated Contractors and the Motivation Condition

The motivation condition for possession of the sense of justice requires that contractors act justly rather than unjustly because they value doing so for its own sake. One might worry, however, that a contractor who has habituated herself into principled preferences would fail to satisfy this condition. Arguably, acting justly rather than unjustly because one values the feeling one associates with doing is not the same thing as acting justly rather than unjustly because one values doing so for itself. For if an agent acted justly rather than unjustly because she valued the feeling associated with doing so, and then ceased to experience this feeling, she would cease to act justly rather than unjustly. Contrastingly, an agent who valued acting justly rather than unjustly for its own sake would continue to so act even were any coincidental association she had managed to forge between so acting and experiencing valued feelings to be disrupted.

This worry misunderstands the motivation of contractors who have habituated themselves into principled preferences. Such contractors do not act justly rather than unjustly because they coincidentally associate doing so with experiencing valued feelings. Rather they act justly because doing so has become of a kind with an activity they value intrinsically, feeling satisfaction. And acting justly rather than unjustly because they value this activity intrinsically, contractors who have habituated themselves into principled preferences satisfy the motivation condition for possession of the sense of justice.

Something might cause any such agent to cease deriving intrinsic satisfaction from acting justly rather than unjustly. In this case, she would no longer value acting justly rather than unjustly intrinsically. Whenever acting justly rather than unjustly prevented such an agent from satisfying her other preferences maximally, she would act unjustly rather than justly. But this is just to say that if an agent who valued acting justly over acting unjustly ceased to do so, she would no longer act justly rather than unjustly in the absence of a sufficiently highly-ranked instrumental preference for so acting. And there is nothing surprising or objectionable about this, at least not within the framework of maximizing rationality.

Habituation and Confusion

One might object to habituation as an account of rational preference revision on the grounds that the deliberation of agents whose preferences change as the result of association are subject to a basic sort of confusion. After all, such agents come to intrinsically prefer an activity by mistaking derivative satisfaction for intrinsic satisfaction. And this being so, perhaps we ought to treat association as a regrettable flaw in the deliberation of merely human agents, and thus as a departure from anything that could be characterized as rational.[12]

In the absence of an argument that association causes agents to do less well at satisfying their preferences than they otherwise would, however, we must classify association as a nonrational process, not an irrational one. And we have characterized contractors as shallowly rational agents, agents whose intrinsic preferences are formed and altered through nonrational processes. Operating within this framework, we have no principled reason for treating agents whose preferences are formed through nonrational association as anything other than rational.[13]

A Limitation on the Scope of the Habituation Model

In explaining how shallowly rational agents might revise their preferences through habituation, we have assumed a particular psychology. And agents not endowed with this psychology cannot revise their preferences as the habituation model describes.

Even rational agents endowed with the appropriate psychology cannot always initiate the habituation we have described. Any time a rational agent preferring X to Y would realize less derivative satisfaction from Y-ing than she would intrinsic satisfaction from X-ing. In all such cases, it would be irrational for her to y when she could X instead, so she would not initiate the habituation which would yield her a preference for Y over X.

And even when agents with the appropriate psychology initiate such a course of habituation, they may fail to complete it successfully. Sometimes, agents lack the time required to develop their target preferences through habituation.[14] Other times, they have the time to habituate themselves, but are too pressured or too distracted to keep track of why they are doing what they are doing. And on the model of habituation we have developed, merely doing Y rather than X repeatedly would not yield an intrinsic preference for Y over X.

In view of these limitations of the habituation model, and of the minimal constraints we have placed on the psychology of contractors, one might worry that some would be psychologically incapable of revising their intrinsic preferences as we have described. And contractors who could not revise their intrinsic preferences are not rationally required to transform themselves.

But there is no reason why all contractors who would benefit from transforming themselves must do so in the same way, using the same resources. And alternative models of preference revision might involve different limitations. By appealing to a number of different models of preference revision, we might be able to explain how any of our contractors, however constituted and situated, could develop principled preferences.

For our present purposes, however, we need not cobble together so sweeping an account of preference revision. For we are engaged here in establishing that despite appearances to the contrary, it is logically possible for our contractors to develop principled preferences through habituation. And given our characterization of contractors, all might be so constituted and so situated that they could revise their intrinsic preferences as we have described. Thus, an appeal to the habituation model, despite its limitations, serves our present purposes adequately.

Conclusion

In this chapter, we have shown that the paradox involved in the claim that shallowly rational agents could revise their intrinsic preferences over actions through habituation is only apparent. In so doing, we have established that were they appropriately constituted, our contractors could acquire an intrinsic preference for acting justly rather than unjustly by repeatedly choosing just over unjust actions for the right reasons. And by establishing this result, we have answered the charge that self-transformation is impossible for rational agents, and thus irrational for our shallowly rational contractors.

Notes

1. Strictly speaking, preferences relate states of affairs, not actions. When I speak of an agent's preferences for action X over action Y, I mean a preference for outcomes in which she does X rather than Y over outcomes in which she does Y rather than X.

2. I thank Duncan MacIntosh for calling this paradox to my attention. It resembles Aristotle's puzzle about habituation and the acquisition of virtue. See Aristotle, *Nicomachean Ethics*, trans. Terence Irwin (Indianapolis: Hackett Publishing Co., 1985), 39–40.

3. We have formulated this paradox in terms of reversing strict preferences, for this form of it is most relevant to our concerns. But the move from strict preference to indifference involves a similar paradox. And among shallowly rational agents, for whom habituation involves costs, so does the move from indifference to strict preference.

4. This idea harks back at least to Aristotle's theory of virtue. See Aristotle, 33–40.

5. This amounts to a form of hedonism. We assume that individuals value very highly a particular sort of pleasant feeling, namely satisfaction. Individuals need not value satisfaction so highly as we assume here to revise their preferences by means of habituation. But the more an individual values satisfaction relative to the other things that she values, the wider the range of circumstances in which she can habituate herself into revised preferences.

6. In this way, someone who initially valued exercise as a mere means might come to find it an intrinsically valuable activity. Less benignly, someone who valued money as a mere means might become the sort of person who values the having of money for its own sake, a miser. Mill invokes a similar associative mechanism in arguing that people's desiring virtue for itself is compatible with his proof of utilitarianism. See John Stuart Mill, *Utilitarianism* (Indianapolis: Hackett Publishing Co., 1979), 35–6.

7. This is consistent with their also believing that under some conditions, such habituation will likely fail to yield an intrinsic preference for X over Y. We discuss some such conditions later in this chapter.

8. This follows from the definition of an instrumental preference.

9. This follows from the form of hedonism we have attributed to agents.

10. Here derivative satisfaction performs the role that pleasure performs in Aristotle's account of habituation. It completes an activity, reinforcing an agent's choice to engage in it. See Aristotle, 275.

11. For instance, I could gain an intrinsic preference for eating Milky Ways over eating Zeros, given my intrinsic preference for eating milk chocolate over eating white chocolate, by discovering that eating Milky Ways is of a kind with the former while eating Zeros is of a kind with the latter.

12. For this objection, I am indebted to an anonymous referee for the *Canadian Journal of Philosophy*.

13. For a defense of our decision to work within the framework of shallow rationality, see Chapter 2.

14. Agents may be able to compensate for a lack of time by substituting mentally "walking through" a certain action repeatedly for performing it repeatedly. Such surrogates for habituation would not always be effective, however, and agents would sometimes lack time even for them.

10

Conclusion: Preferring Justice

Our argument for the rationality of self-transformation constitutes a fundamental justification of the sense of justice for most members of our community. It picks out reasons sufficient to justify maintaining such a disposition to most of us which do not derive from the sense of justice itself. By appealing to this argument, we can answer the skeptical worries about the sense of justice from which we began. For this argument implies that the sense of justice, far from being an instrument of social control, is something most of us require in order to do as well as possible at achieving whatever ends we have apart from the end of acting justly rather than unjustly.

The Dangers of Empiricism

But this argument contains a large number of empirical premises. Perhaps, despite our arguments to the contrary, one of these premises is both descriptively inaccurate and more advantageous to the true transformer than to the faker strategy. And perhaps it could be shown that were this premise replaced with a more appropriate one, our argument for the rationality of self-transformation would fail. Would this not invalidate our conclusion about the rationality of maintaining the sense of justice?

Of course it would. But being shown to rest on a false premise would invalidate the conclusion of any argument, so this possibility does not reveal any flaw in our justification of the sense of justice. And besides, even were our argument for the rationality of self-transformation to fail in this manner, it would still advance our project considerably. To notice this is to define a fallback position for ourselves.

A Fallback Position

Suppose that our argument for the rationality of self-transformation failed in just the manner discussed above. Such an argument would, despite its reliance on a descriptively inaccurate premise favoring the true transformer over the faker strategy, constitute a successful possibility proof of the rationality of self-transformation. It would establish the existence of a set of possible conditions under which rationality requires most of us to maintain the sense of justice. And while such a possibility proof does not itself constitute a fundamental justification of the sense of justice, it would nonetheless advance our project.

Given conflicting preferences and moderate scarcity, rules of justice would require individuals to constrain their attempts to satisfy their preferences some of the time. And the sense of justice would dispose individuals to follow these rules. Claiming that it is never rational for an individual to constrain her attempts to satisfy her preferences, one might argue that rationality would never require an individual to dispose herself to such constraint, so it would never require her to maintain the sense of justice.

Committed to such radical skepticism about the sense of justice, an individual would regard possession of such a disposition as a liability. And she would regard our justification of the sense of justice as so much dangerous ideology, to be resisted at all costs. Hence, unrefuted, radical skepticism about the sense of justice can render individuals extremely unreceptive to our project.

A successful possibility proof of the rationality of self-transformation would refute such skepticism. Confronted with a proof that there exist conditions under which maintaining the sense of justice is rational, individuals cannot simply dismiss the sense of justice as a liability. They must recognize that maintaining such a disposition is rational in some situations, and consider the possibility that it may be so in their own.

Besides refuting a form of skepticism threatening our project, a successful possibility proof of the rationality of self-transformation would advance our project more directly. Such a proof would reveal a set of conditions under which maintaining the sense of justice is rational for individuals. And when these conditions do not obtain, this revelation can guide attempts to reshape conditions so as to render maintaining the sense of justice rational for individuals.

Thus, even were our argument for the rationality of self-transformation to fail in the manner we have described, it would still accomplish something significant. For it would establish that a fundamental justification of the sense of justice is available to us, and indicate how we might avail ourselves of such a justification. And for those of us concerned to reconcile possession of the sense of justice with the requirements of rationality, this is the next best thing to a successful fundamental justification of this disposition.

While it is comforting to know that we have such a fallback position available, the premises of our argument for the rationality of self-transformation are either neutral between the faker and true transformer strategies, or exaggerate our circumstances in ways favoring the former over the latter. And this insures that no substitution into our argument of premises describing our present circumstances more accurately could weaken its conclusion. Thus, so long as our circumstances do not change drastically, we need not retreat to the fallback position we have defined.

Our circumstances might, of course, change drastically, forcing us (or our descendants) to substitute new premises into our argument for the rationality of self-transformation. And in this case, we (or they) might have to retreat to the above fallback position. But this possibility does not indicate a flaw in our justification of the sense of justice. To the contrary, since having such a disposition is not an asset in all possible situations, an *a priori* justification of the sense of justice would be deeply suspect.

A Conditional Success

But even if the premises of our argument are descriptively accurate and favor the faker over the true transformer strategy, our success at providing most members of our community with a fundamental justification of the sense of justice is conditional on several things.

First, if there exist conceptions of justice which preclude individuals from developing the sense of justice, our justification of the sense of justice to individuals is conditional on their not subscribing to such a conception.[1] For developing the sense of justice would prevent individuals subscribing to such a conception from implementing it, and individuals who fail to implement their conception of justice can realize no benefit from it. Thus, were we to exchange our conception of justice for such a conception, maintaining the sense of justice would no longer be collectively rational for us.

Second, our success is conditional on the adequacy of the list of solutions to the prisoner's dilemma (*PD*) we relied upon in generating the joint strategies available to contractors. Were a new means for resolving *PD*s to become available to us, then the list of joint strategies available to contractors would have to reflect this. And facing an expanded list of joint strategies, the transformer strategy might no longer be collectively rational for our contractors, or by implication, for us.

And third, our success is conditional on the adequacy of our short list of decision rules for choice under uncertainty. Were anyone to propose other such rules no less plausible than the rules on our short list, we would have to expand this list accordingly. And with the addition of any decision rules to our short list, the true transformer strategy might no longer maximize decision value for typical contractors, or by implication, for typical members of our community.

But that we must so condition our conclusion about the rationality of maintaining the sense of justice in these ways is fitting. For whether rationality requires individuals to maintain the sense of justice is relative to their conception of justice, their available options, and an account of rationality. So substantial changes to our conception of justice, our available means of resolving *PD*s, or our account of rationality require us to rethink the connection between instrumental rationality and being just.

A Limited Success

Jean Hampton develops a criticism of instrumental justifications of morality which suggests that the success of our justification of the sense of justice is not only conditional, but limited.[2]

Hampton points out that instrumental justifications of moral constraints provide individuals with no reason to respect those with whom they have no interest in cooperating—the very old, the infirm, the severely handicapped, members of future generations, and members of societies much less developed than their own. She suggests that for this reason, instrumental justifications of moral constraints fail in a very serious way to capture the nature of morality.

One might think that our instrumental justification of the sense of justice fails in this way. But it would fail to provide individuals with reason to treat the easily-dominated justly only within communities governed by conceptions of justice which do not require that such individuals be treated justly. Where rules of justice require that individuals treat the easily-dominated justly, those to whom we have successfully justified the sense of justice would have reason to treat such individuals justly. Their own preferences would provide such individuals exhibiting the sense of justice with such reason. And any such individuals not exhibiting the sense of justice have reason to develop one, and thus to treat the easily-dominated justly as a means of doing so. Thus, that our justification of the sense of justice appeals to instrumental rationality does not limit the class of individuals that those to whom we have justified this disposition have reason to treat justly.

It does, however, impose a limitation of another sort upon our justification of the sense of justice. For as we have seen, there are some who gain more by exploiting their fellows than by cooperating with them. And we cannot justify the sense of justice to such by appealing to instrumental rationality. Thus, our reliance on instrumental rationality limits the class of individuals to whom we can justify the sense of justice.

We cannot justify the sense of justice to malevolent members of our community. For we cannot generalize the conclusion that rationality requires nontuistic contractors to maintain the sense of justice to malevolent members of our audience. Having a disposition to treat others justly rather than unjustly would prevent those who rank frustrating the preferences of others higher than satisfying their own nontuistic or benevolent preferences from maximizing utility.

Nor can we justify the sense of justice to gifted members of our community. For the argument we have developed implies that gifted contractors ought to purge themselves of the sense of justice so that they might exploit their fellows when it pays enough to do so. By appealing to this argument, we justify faking to gifted members of our community, not developing the sense of justice.

In the Lion's Den

One might find this failure to justify the sense of justice to the gifted troubling. For it is lack of the sense of justice in just such individuals that poses the greatest danger to just individuals.[3] Among contractors constituted as we have assumed, the .25 most elusive individuals ought to do without the sense of justice. And one might worry that rationality cannot require typical members of such a community to maintain the sense of justice when so many of the most dangerous of their fellows are poised to exploit them.

We have argued that under a sufficiently effective enforcement mechanism, it is rational for typical members of such a community to maintain the sense of justice even under such conditions. This reply, however, just pushes the above worry up a level. One might be no less worried about a community's capacity for maintaining an effective enforcement mechanism when the most elusive .25 of its members lack the sense of justice. For were so many members of a community to refrain from supporting their enforcement mechanism, its effectiveness would be undermined. And under an enforcement mechanism substantially less effective than we have supposed, maintaining the sense of justice would not be rational.

But our argument implies that fully .25 of the most elusive members of a community ought to fake only when each is sufficiently gifted to expect more as a faker than as a true transformer. Where the .25 most elusive members of a community are not all so gifted, fewer than .25 of them are rationally required to become fakers.

And our argument implies that fully .25 of the most elusive members of a community ought to fake only under conditions of opacity. As contractors become more translucent, true transformers become better at avoiding being exploited, and fakers become worse at exploiting others and at avoiding their enforcement mechanism when they do so. Where the members of a community are sufficiently translucent, fewer than .25 of them are rationally required to become fakers.

If we turned out to be less gifted or more translucent, on the whole, than our contractors, then our argument would justify the sense of justice to many gifted as well as typical individuals. And the more members of our community to whom we justify the sense of justice, the fewer would refuse to support our enforcement mechanism, and the lower the odds of its effectiveness being undermined enough to render maintaining the sense of justice irrational for us.

We cannot count on our being any less gifted or any more translucent than our contractors, however. For how gifted we turn out to be, and how translucent we turn out to be, are entirely contingent matters. But though we may have failed to justify the sense of justice to the gifted members of our community, we have shown that all such have reason to support an enforcement mechanism providing all, including themselves, with an incentive to comply with the rules of justice. This follows from the conjunction of our argument that choosing the transformer over the policer strategy is collectively rational for our contractors and our argument that they could and would do what is required to empower a transformer enforcement mechanism. Thus, we need not worry that the gifted members of our community would refuse to support our enforcement mechanism, rendering maintenance of the sense of justice irrational for the rest of us.[4]

We cannot generalize this conclusion to those who rank frustrating the preferences of others higher than satisfying their own nontuistic or benevolent preferences. But such profoundly malevolent individuals are, within our own community at least, rare. With all but such members of our community supporting our enforcement mechanism, its effectiveness would be uncompromised. And, as we have already argued, rationality requires typical members of our community who are not so malevolent to maintain the sense of justice when our enforcement mechanism is operating at full effectiveness. Thus, our failure to justify the sense of justice to the most profoundly malevolent members of our community does not render it irrational for the rest of us to maintain such a disposition.

Grounds for Disappointment?

From the perspective of most of us, we would have done better to provide a fundamental justification of the sense of justice to more members of our community than we have. For most of us exhibit the sense of justice already. And those of us exhibiting the sense of justice do better the more of our fellows exhibit such a disposition. Thus, for most of us, our failure to justify the sense of justice to all within our community would appear grounds for disappointment.

Some have suggested that we should not be disappointed by our inability to rationalize morality to malevolent individuals because doing so is a hopeless task.[7] But even if we have no hope of rationalizing the sense of justice to malevolent individuals, we may yet aspire to justifying this disposition to them fundamentally. And despite our failure to rationalize the sense of justice to gifted individuals, we may harbor similar aspirations with respect to them. Thus, even if we have no hope of rationalizing the sense of justice to the malevolent and the gifted, it does not follow that disappointment at the limited success of our project is groundless.

But were we to provide a fundamental justification of the sense of justice to all within our community, we could expect each to maintain such a disposition. And if each did so, it would never be rational for any of us to act unjustly. In this case, however, we would have difficulty making sense of injustice. Unjust actions would be as baffling to us as irrational actions. But they are not always, or even usually, so. Because it enables us to preserve our everyday distinction between irrationality and injustice, one might argue, our failure to fundamentally justify the sense of justice to everyone within our community is a virtue of our account, not grounds for disappointment.[5]

Were we engaged in explaining moral practices within our own community, this would be true. For putatively rational members of our community are tempted by injustice, and sometimes they succumb. But we are engaged in justifying the sense of justice to members of our community, not in explaining their current moral practices.[6] And if our current moral practices are less than optimal, then it may not be a virtue of a fundamental justification of the sense of justice that it would preserve our everyday moral distinctions. Thus, disappointment at our limited success at providing members of our community with a fundamental justification of the sense of justice cannot be dismissed on explanatory grounds.

If we assumed away the complications introduced into our own dealings by malevolence and giftedness, we could provide every member of our community with an argument that she ought to maintain the sense of justice. But an appeal to such an argument would justify the sense of justice to the malevolent and the gifted no more effectively than the one we have developed. For such individuals would (rightly) deny that such an argument establishes anything at all about what they have reason to do.

From these last two observations, it is tempting to conclude that fundamentally justifying the sense of justice to all within our community is impossible in principle, both explaining and excusing our failure to do so. But this would be a mistake.

Rawls claims that a particular conception of justice is justified to all members of a community when there is an *overlapping consensus* on this conception.[8] Such a consensus has been achieved when each of the divergent conceptions of the good within a community affirms the same conception of justice for reasons recognized by each as valid. In such a consensus, all affirm the same conception of justice, although each may do so for different reasons.

An appeal to something like an overlapping consensus explains how we might provide a fundamental justification of the sense of justice to everyone within our community, even the malevolent and the gifted.[9] To do so, we would have to appeal to reasons for maintaining the sense of justice other than those revealed by our appeal to instrumental rationality. By yoking the right combination of such appeals to our appeal to instrumental rationality, we might be able to provide each member of our community with reasons she would recognize for maintaining the sense of justice. And if none of these derived from the sense of justice itself, then having successfully cultivated such an overlapping consensus, we would have provided every member of our community with a fundamental justification of this disposition.

While such an overlapping consensus is possible, there are significant obstacles to extending our fundamental justification of the sense of justice into one. Some of the malevolent and the gifted might not have any practical commitments capable of yielding reasons for maintaining the sense of justice. Others might have such commitments, but not of the sort which could ground a fundamental justification of this disposition. If malevolent and gifted member of our community had such practical commitments, these might yet be incompatible with one another, or with a commitment to instrumental rationality. If an appeal to disparate practical commitments turned out to be internally coherent, its different components might yet alienate different elements of our pluralistic community. And finally, even if we managed to cobble together a set of appeals providing each of us with a fundamental justification of the sense of justice, the constant changes in the composition of our community make it unlikely that such an overlapping consensus could long endure.

In the face of all of these obstacles, our chances of extending our fundamental justification of the sense of justice into such an overlapping consensus are vanishingly small. Indeed, we are unlikely to approach this ideal any more closely than we have here even if we try. Nonetheless, it is possible to provide a fundamental justification of the sense of justice to more of us than we have here. And for this reason, we cannot dismiss disappointment at our failure to do so as inappropriate.

Any such disappointment evinced by members of our audience, however, should be leavened by considerable appreciation for what we have achieved. For we have established that most of us have what we recognize as sufficient reason, quite apart from any considerations provided by the sense of justice itself, for preferring justice to injustice intrinsically. And having accomplished even this much, we are helping to diffuse alienation from the sense of justice within our community, benefitting virtually all of us. Those disappointed that we have not achieved more have an incentive to attempt an even more inclusive fundamental justification of the sense of justice, either by building upon what we have accomplished here, or by some other means entirely.

Notes

1. For a discussion of this possibility, see Chapter 2.

2. For this criticism, see Jean Hampton, "Two Faces of Contractarian Thought," in *Contractarianism and Rational Choice: Essays on David Gauthier's Morals By Agreement*, ed. Peter Vallentyne (New York: Cambridge University Press, 1991), 31–55.

3. I owe this objection to Greg Kavka.

4. In thinking about this worry, I learned much from Jan Narveson's remarks in "Reason in Ethics—or Reason Versus Ethics?" in *Morality, Reason, and Truth, New Essays on the Foundations of Ethics*, ed. David Copp and David Zimmerman (Totowa: Rowman and Allanheld, 1985), 228–50.

5. I learned this argument from Jan Narveson, who deploys it in defending his attempt to reconcile rationality and morality. See Narveson, 247–8.

6. For a detailed discussion of the distinction between explanation and justification, see Alan Nelson, "Explanation and Justification in Political Philosophy," *Ethics* 97 (1986): 154–76.

7. See Gregory S. Kavka, "The Reconciliation Project," in *Morality, Reason, and Truth, New Essays on the Foundations of Ethics*, ed. David Copp and David Zimmerman (Totowa: Rowman and Allanheld, 1985), 297–319. See also Narveson, 246–7.

8. See John Rawls, "The Idea of an Overlapping Consensus," *Oxford Journal of Legal Studies* 7 (1987): 1–25.

9. This explanation assumes that all members of our community agree on a core conception of justice. For discussion of this assumption, see Chapter 2.

References

Ainslie, George. (1975). "Specious Reward: A Behavioral Theory of Impulsiveness and Impulse Control." *Psychological Bulletin* 82: 463–96.

Aristotle. (1985). *Nicomachean Ethics*, trans. Terence Irwin. Indianapolis: Hackett Publishing Co.

Axelrod, Robert. (1984). *The Evolution of Cooperation*. New York: Basic Books, Inc.

Binmore, K., and P. Dasgupta. (1986). *Economic Organizations as Games*. New York: Basil Blackwell Press.

Brandt, Richard B. (1979). *A Theory of the Good and the Right*. New York: Clarendon Press.

Bratman, Michael. (1989). *Intention, Plans, and Practical Reason*. Cambridge: Harvard University Press.

Brink, David O. (1989). *Moral Realism and the Foundations of Ethics*. New York: Cambridge University Press.

Broome, John. (1992). Review of *Rationality and Dynamic Choice: Foundational Explorations*. *Ethics* 102: 666–8.

Campbell, Richmond. (1985). "Background for the Uninitiated." In *Paradoxes of Rationality and Cooperation*, ed. Richmond Campbell and Lanning Sowden. Vancouver: University of British Columbia Press, 3–41.

Danielson, Peter. (1992). *Artificial Morality*. London: Routledge.

Darwall, Stephen L. (1983). *Impartial Reason*. London: Cornell University Press.

———. (1992). "Internalism and Agency." *Philosophical Perspectives* 6: 155–74.

Davis, Lawrence. (1985). "Prisoners, Paradox, and Rationality." In *Paradoxes of Rationality and Cooperation*, ed. Richmond Campbell and Lanning Sowden. Vancouver: University of British Columbia Press, 45–59.

Eisenstadt, S. N., and L. Roniger. (1984). *Persons, Clients, and Friends: Interpersonal Relations and the Structure of Trust in Society*. Cambridge: Cambridge University Press.

Elster, John. (1979). *Ulysses and the Sirens*. Cambridge: Cambridge University Press.

Federal Bureau of Investigation. (1986–95). *Uniform Crime Reports for the United States*. Washington, D. C.: U. S. Government Printing Office.

Frank, Robert. (1988). *Passions Within Reason*. New York: W. W. Norton and Co.

Gauthier, David. (1975). "Reason and Maximization." *Canadian Journal of Philosophy* 4: 411–33.

———. (1986). *Morals by Agreement*. New York: Oxford University Press.

———. (1988). "Morality, Rational Choice, and Semantic Representation." *Social Philosophy and Policy* 5: 173–221.

———. (1988–89). "In the Neighborhood of the Newcomb-Predictor." *Proceedings of The Aristotelian Society* 89: 179–94.

———. (1993). "Value, Reasons, and the Sense of Justice." In *Value, Welfare, and Morality,* ed. R. G. Frey and Christopher Morris. Cambridge: Cambridge University Press, 180–208.

———. "Resolute Choice and Rational Deliberation: A Critique and a Defence." Unpublished.

Gilbert, Margaret. (1989). "Rationality and Salience." *Philosophical Studies* 57: 61–77.

Hampton, Jean. (1986). *Hobbes and the Social Contract Tradition.* Cambridge: Cambridge University Press.

———. (1987). "Free-Rider Problems in the Production of Collective Goods." *Economics and Philosophy* 3: 245–73.

———. (1991). "Two Faces of Contractarian Thought." In *Contractarianism and Rational Choice: Essays on David Gauthier's Morals By Agreement,* ed. Peter Vallentyne. New York: Cambridge University Press, 31–55.

Harsanyi, John. (1967). "Games with Incomplete Information Played by 'Bayesian' Players, Parts I, II, and III." *Management Science* 14: 159–82, 320–34, 486–502.

Hobbes, Thomas. (1988). *Leviathan,* ed. C. B. MacPherson. New York: Penguin Books.

Hume, David. (1975). *An Enquiry Concerning the Principles of Morals,* ed. L. A. Selby-Bigge. Oxford: Oxford University Press.

Kavka, Gregory S. (1980). "Deterrence, Utility, and Rational Choice." *Theory and Decision* 12: 41–60.

———. (1985). "The Reconciliation Project." In *Morality, Reason, and Truth, New Essays on the Foundations of Ethics,* ed. David Copp and David Zimmerman. Totowa: Rowman and Allanheld, 297–319.

———. (1986). *Hobbesian Moral and Political Theory.* Princeton: Princeton University Press.

———. (1987). Review of *Morals by Agreement. Mind* 96: 117–21.

Kymlicka, Will. (1988). "Liberalism and Communitarianism." *Canadian Journal of Philosophy* 18: 181–204.

Lewis, David. (1969). *Convention: A Philosophical Study.* Cambridge: Harvard University Press.

Luce, R. D., and H. Raiffa. (1957). *Games and Decisions.* New York: John Wiley & Sons, Inc.

MacIntosh, Duncan. (1988). "Libertarian Agency and Rational Morality: Action-Theoretic Objections To Gauthier's Dispositional Solution of the Compliance Problem." *The Southern Journal of Philosophy* 26: 499–525.

———. (1989). "Two Gauthiers?" *Dialogue* 28: 43–61.

———. (1991). "McClennen's Early Co-operative Solution to the Prisoner's Dilemma." *The Southern Journal of Philosophy* 39: 341–58.

———. (1991). "Co-operative Solutions to the Prisoner's Dilemma." *Philosophical Studies* 64: 309–21.

———. (1991). "Preference's Progress: Rational Self-Alteration and the Rationality of Morality." *Dialogue* 30: 3–32.

————. (1991). "Retaliation Rationalized: Gauthier's Solution to the Deterrence Dilemma." *Pacific Philosophical Quarterly* 72: 9–32.

————. (1992). "Preference-Revision and the Paradoxes of Instrumental Rationality." *Canadian Journal of Philosophy* 22: 474–95.

————. (1992). "Buridan and the Circumstances of Justice (On the Implications of the Rational Unsolvability of Certain Co-ordination Problems)." *Pacific Philosophical Quarterly* 73: 150–73.

————. (1993). "Persons and the Satisfaction of Preferences: Problems in the Rational Kinematics of Values." *The Journal of Philosophy* 90: 163–80.

————. (1996). "Categorically Rational Preferences and the Structure of Morality." In *Vancouver Studies in Cognitive Science*, Vol. 7, ed. Peter Danielson. Vancouver: Oxford University Press: 281–301.

MacIntyre, Alasdair. (1981). *After Virtue: A Study in Moral Theory*. London: Duckworth Press.

McClennen, E. F. (1990). *Rationality and Dynamic Choice: Foundational Explorations*. Cambridge: Cambridge University Press.

Mill, John Stuart. (1979). *Utilitarianism*. Indianapolis: Hackett Publishing Co.

Morris, Christopher. (1991). "Moral Standing and Rational-Choice Contractarianism." In *Contractarianism and Rational Choice*, ed. Peter Vallentyne. Cambridge: Cambridge University Press, 76–95.

Myerson, R. (1978). "Refinements of the Nash Equilibrium Concept." *International Journal of Game Theory* 7: 73–80.

Nagel, Thomas. (1970). *The Possibility of Altruism*. Oxford: Oxford University Press.

Narveson, Jan. (1985). "Reason in Ethics—or Reason versus Ethics?" In *Morality, Reason, and Truth: New Essays on the Foundations of Ethics*, ed. David Copp and David Zimmerman. Totowa: Rowman and Allanheld, 228–50.

————. (1988). *The Libertarian Idea*. Philadelphia: Temple University Press.

Nelson, Alan. (1986). "Explanation and Justification in Political Philosophy." *Ethics* 97: 154–76.

————. (1988). "Economic Rationality and Morality." *Philosophy and Public Affairs* 17: 149–66.

Nozick, Robert. (1974). *Anarchy, State and Utopia*. New York: Basic Books, Inc.

————. (1981). *Philosophical Explanations*. Cambridge: Harvard University Press.

————. (1993). *The Nature of Rationality*. Princeton: Princeton University Press.

Olson, Mancur, Jr. (1965). *The Logic of Collective Action*. Cambridge: Harvard University Press.

Orwell, George. (1949). *1984*. New York: Harcourt, Brace, and Co.

Parfit, Derek. (1984). *Reasons and Persons*. Oxford: Oxford University Press.

Plato. (1992). *The Republic*, trans. G. M. A. Grube. Indianapolis: Hackett Publishing Co.

Rawls, John. (1971). *A Theory of Justice*. Cambridge: Harvard University Press.

————. (1987). "The Idea of an Overlapping Consensus." *Oxford Journal of Legal Studies* 7: 1–25.

Sandel, Michael. (1982). *Liberalism and the Limits of Justice*. Cambridge: Cambridge University Press.

Sayre-McCord, Geoffrey. (1989). "Deception and Reasons to Be Moral." *American Philosophical Quarterly* 26: 181–95.

Schelling, Thomas. (1960). *The Strategy of Conflict.* Cambridge: Harvard University Press.

Schmidtz, David. (1991). *The Limits of Government.* Boulder: Westview Press.

———. (1995). *Rational Choice and Moral Agency.* Princeton: Princeton University Press.

Selten, Reinhard. (1975). "Re-examination of the Perfectness Concept for Equilibrium Points in Extensive Games." *International Journal of Game Theory* 4: 25–35.

Sen, Amartya. (1967). "Isolation, Assurance, and the Social Rate of Discount." *Quarterly Journal of Economics* 81: 112–24.

———. (1970). *Collective Choice and Social Welfare.* San Francisco: Holden Day, Inc.

———. (1974). "Choice, Orderings, and Morality." In *Practical Reasoning,* ed. Stephan Korner. Oxford: Basil Blackwell Press, 54–67.

Skyrms, Brian. (1990). *The Dynamics of Rational Deliberation.* Cambridge: Harvard University Press.

Sugden, Robert. (1990). "Contractarianism and Norms." *Ethics* 100: 768–86.

Verbeek, Bruno. "On the Rationality of Intentions." Unpublished.

Vorabej, Mark. (1986). "Gauthier on Deterrence." *Dialogue* 25: 471–6.

Williams, Bernard. (1976). "Persons, Character, and Morality." In *The Identities of Persons,* ed. Amelie Oksenberg Rorty. Berkeley: University of California Press, 197–216.

Index